"Hope is water to someone suffering with depression. In her book, *30 Days of Hope for Dealing with Depression*, Brenda Poinsett waters our souls with fresh life, helping us to see that depression is not the end but an opportunity for a new beginning. Believe there is life after depression. For the next 30 days, take Brenda's hand and allow her to offer you the tools and hope she discovered on her own journey to freedom from depression. For years, I have encouraged many women battling depression; I would recommend this devotional to any one of them."

—Patty Mason, founder of Liberty in Christ Ministries,
author of *Experiencing Joy: Strategies for Living
a Joy Filled Life* and *The Power of Hope*

"*30 Days of Hope for Dealing with Depression* by Brenda Poinsett belongs in every pastor's office and on every guidance counselor's and Christian mental health professional's desk. It will surely offer hope to anyone dealing with depression and affirm the fact that they are not alone and that God has not forgotten them. Using Scripture to support what she says, she displays how depression has always been with us and helps battle the stigma and associated shame of depression. She imparts wisdom, hope, and uses a good dose of humor to deliver her powerful message, and I salute her. I will be buying multiple copies for use in my own practice."

—Myla P. Erwin, certified biblical counselor,
certified advanced life coach

"Brenda Poinsett has done it again. Drawing from her own experience with depression and her keen insights from Scripture, she points fellow sufferers down the path toward hope. Along the way she provides quotes and excerpts from a wide range of authors that in themselves offer a guide for further exploration. Brenda consistently points toward a personal faith in Jesus Christ 'indelibly printed . . . on my soul' as a key component in this rediscovery of hope. In her honest and transparent chronicle of the causes and containment of her own depression, she also advocates honest, transparent praying since nothing can shock the God who made us and who loves us. Indeed this kind of raw, spiritual outburst itself may give rise to hope. Practical advice abounds when she describes how God uses people in and through their illness. Reading through these 30 days of reflections can prepare any reader to begin the journey toward the recovery of hope."

—Dr. Franklin R. Dumond, director of congregational
ministries, General Association of General Baptists

"The author's vivid, genuine, and vulnerable devotions help
normalize   The author
brings   state."

—Matt Gildeh   Delta Counseling

"Using practical wisdom and personal experience, Brenda Poinsett offers a compassionate and transparent look at depression, one that's sure to bring hope to many."

—Jennifer Slattery, founder of Wholly Loved Ministries and author of *Restoring Love*

"No one chooses depression. With no respecter of persons, depression chooses its victims and cloaks them in a paralyzing fog of hopelessness. Brenda Poinsett, who found her way out of the clutches of depression, presents genuine hope in 30 days. Her parable of a withered fern in a clay pot that against all odds came back to life parallels her personal journey from hopelessness to healing. Each day, Brenda uses God's Word to shine a beacon of light into the dark places of the soul, soothe the wounded spirit, and offer tools to break the tenacious grip of depression on one's life. With each day, you too will 'begin to believe that life can get better not because of who we are but because of who God is.'"

—Debby Akerman, national WMU® president emerita

"Brenda Poinsett's research and personal experience with depression make this book an invaluable resource for anyone struggling with depression. As I read this book, I kept thinking of numerous clients I've worked with over the years that could benefit from reading this book. Brenda truly lays out a road map that can empower a person to assist in their own recovery."

—Mary M. (Peggy) Brooks, licensed marriage and family therapist

"Brenda Poinsett comes alongside her readers with a combination of wisdom gained from personal experience, others' stories, biblical examples, study, insight, and thoughtful questions, and she gently guides them one step at a time toward hope. *30 Days of Hope for Dealing with Depression* is a warmly written, refreshing book. It's an encouraging and much-needed resource for those who are depressed."

—Twila Belk, writer, speaker, and author of *Raindrops from Heaven: Gentle Reminders of God's Power, Presence, and Purpose*

"Depression is more than 'feeling down' or 'having the blues.' It is also not hopeless. Through her experiences, and that of others, Brenda Poinsett offers more than a few pat answers. *30 Days of Hope for Dealing with Depression* shows us the light, even when all we can see is a pinpoint, of God's care and love through the valley of the shadow. This devotional encourages those with depression and their loved ones. It will not only be on my shelf, so I can return to it when I'm in that valley, but I will also share it with others. Thank you, Brenda, for caring enough to be vulnerable and sharing your journey to the end of the tunnel."

—Susan K. Stewart, author and speaker

GIFTS OF HOPE SERIES

30 DAYS OF HOPE

FOR DEALING WITH DEPRESSION

BRENDA POINSETT

NEW HOPE
PUBLISHERS
Gospel-Centered. Missions-Driven.

BIRMINGHAM, ALABAMA

New Hope® Publishers
PO Box 12065
Birmingham, AL 35202-2065
NewHopePublishers.com
New Hope Publishers is a division of WMU®.

Library of Congress Cataloging-in-Publication Data
Names: Poinsett, Brenda, author.
Title: 30 days of hope for dealing with depression / Brenda Poinsett.
Other titles: Thirty days of hope for dealing with depression
Description: First [edition]. | Birmingham : New Hope Publishers, 2017.
Identifiers: LCCN 2017006350 | ISBN 9781625915207 (permabind)
Subjects: LCSH: Depression, Mental—Religious aspects—Christianity. |
    Depressed persons—Religious life.
Classification: LCC BV4910.34 .P64 2017 | DDC 248.8/625—dc23
LC record available at https://lccn.loc.gov/2017006350

ISBN-13: 978-1-62591-520-7

N174118 • 0517 • 1M1

To Myla, who understands.

TABLE OF CONTENTS

ACKNOWLEDGMENTS

I'm so glad to have had the opportunity to write a book offering 30 days of hope for those who are depressed. Based on the reactions I get when I speak to groups about depression, its message is much needed. It's not unusual for me to get this response: "Thank you for being honest enough to say Christians can get depressed."

I'm grateful to New Hope Publishers for agreeing with me that Christians do get depressed and giving me the chance to write words of encouragement. I'm grateful to Mark Bethea, Sarah Doss, Melissa Hall, Reagan Jackson, Maegan Roper, Tina Atchenson, and others of the New Hope team who believed in the book and saw it through to completion.

I also appreciate the help of my husband, Bob Poinsett; my sister, Judy Mills; and my son, Ben Poinsett. They read the manuscript day-by-day, found errors, and gave me valuable feedback and encouragement. I'm sure the book reads better because of their help.

Janet Hofer showed support with lovely, weekly handmade cards letting me know she was praying for me. Others prayed too, and I say thanks to Jim Poinsett, Margie Kruse, Barb Speer, Naomi Richardson, Janet Palmer, Pat Bearden, Betty Dockery, Mary Rose Fox, Annette Huber, Sue Johnson, Julie Andresen, Cheryl Stahlman, Virgie Finn, Jan Turner, Myrna Turner, Kristi Neace, Valerie Howe, and Mary Ann Paille. If I've missed a name, please forgive me, and let me know so I can thank you in person.

All of you, in your own way, added to the richness of the book's content. Let's now pray that many people will find some light in the darkness of their depression.

INTRODUCTION

A RE YOU feeling sad? Have you lost interest in what you used to do? Do you feel like life will never be the same again? If your answer is yes, then I trust this book will be an encouragement to you. Writing it was encouragement for me, for it reminded me of the many lessons I've learned in studying depression, talking with others about their experiences, and seeing what the Bible has to say.

I was depressed before I knew there was such a thing as depression. Oh, I had used the word many times, but I didn't know there was an identifiable condition known as depression. Once I learned this, I began to study depression. I wanted to understand it and help myself recover.

What I learned was so insightful that I wanted to share it with my Sunday School class at one of our outside-the-church monthly gatherings. After announcing we'd be discussing depression, I had more people show up than ever before. *Hmmm*, I thought, *maybe this is something people need help with.* So I began speaking about it.

I went to conferences and workshops and shared what I learned. People always wanted to talk with me afterwards, to tell me about their experiences. I'm not a mental health professional; I haven't been trained in counseling, but I could listen, and listening encourages hopefulness.

I also began writing about depression. I wrote *Understanding a Woman's Depression* and then *Why Do I Feel This Way?*

While studying, speaking, and writing, I memorized the symptoms of depression. Perhaps this is why I recognized some symptoms in various Bible characters. When they had three or more of the symptoms, I labeled them in my teaching—and now in this book—as being depressed, although the Bible doesn't actually refer to them that way. Depression as a term didn't develop until 1600, but judging by symptoms I saw, certain Bible characters were depressed. These observations turned into a book called *When Saints Sing the Blues: Understanding Depression through the Lives of Job, Naomi, Paul, and Others.*

The common denominator of those I've talked with and those I've written about is the need for hope, which is why I've written this book. In it, I've included the lessons I learned from a faith perspective, trusting they will nurture your hope.

You may be wondering, *Well, what kind of depression are you addressing in this book?* That's a good question because depression has many names: clinical depression, major depressive disorder, mood disorder, brain disorder, circumstantial depression, and systemic depression, to list a few. For this book, though, I'm not into specific labels except to say I'll always be referencing *unipolar* depression (characterized by a down mood) and not *bipolar* depression (characterized by extreme moods of highs and lows). I purposely did not identify whether I'm writing for those who have been diagnosed with depression or those who are depressed but haven't been diagnosed. I'm writing to the person who if he or she passed a book in a bookstore and saw the word "depressed" would say, "That's me." To you, I would say, "I have something for you. Here's 30 days of hope!"

WHEN HOPE SPROUTS

*But we have this treasure in jars of clay . . . We always
carry around in our body the death of Jesus, so that
the life of Jesus may also be revealed in our body.*

—2 Corinthians 4:7–10 NIV

WHEN my neighbor told me she was going to have a garage sale, I feigned interest. What did I need with more stuff? I felt overwhelmed by what I already had.

While we talked, I spotted a clay flowerpot among the sale items. Now my interest picked up a little. I'm a plant person, so I'm always on the lookout for inexpensive pots.

When the sale got underway the next day, I walked over to the neighbor's. I picked up the pot to see if it had any cracks. I saw that not only was the pot clay, but so was the soil. No Miracle Gro in view here! Long ago the soil had seen its last bit of moisture. Even if I had wanted to plant something in it, I doubted a seed could have penetrated the concrete-like soil.

Interestingly, the whispery, feathery remnants of a plumosa fern remained in the pot. Not green and growing but brown and fragile. I pinched off a piece, and it immediately crumbled in my hand. A plumosa fern is not a plant you often see. Too bad someone didn't nourish it or keep it watered.

I bought the flowerpot and carried it home. I vowed that when I felt better, I would dig out the hardened soil, scrape out the mineral deposits, wash the pot, put in new soil, and plant something in it. Eventually something green would again thrive in the clay pot. It wouldn't be anytime soon, though, because I just didn't have it in me to exert that much energy. I was depressed and had been for some time.

I sat the pot down on the concrete floor under our covered patio. In the days following, as I went in and out of the back door, I often glanced at the lifeless plant. Each time I thought, *That's me. Dry. Brittle. Disintegrating.* Tears are a common symptom of depression, but I hadn't been crying. In fact, I wished that I could. Perhaps then something could be released in me that would let the vitality of life swell up within me as it once had. As it was, I was going through the motions of everyday life, taking care of my children and keeping up with my responsibilities, but I was doing it all very slowly. It was like my feet were set in hard clay; every step was weighty and took a tremendous amount of effort. When it rained, I was glad. This meant I didn't have to do outside work. I stayed inside, brooding and listening to the wind.

A few days later, while carrying in groceries from the car, a little slip of green in the clay pot caught my eye. Could it be a big green bug? Perhaps a tiny green snake? After putting away the groceries, I went back to the patio. I picked up the clay pot, and there near the base of the dry fern was green growth! The plant that gave all appearances of being dead was alive! Apparently enough raindrops had blown onto the patio to dampen the pot's hardened soil. The moisture of those few drops ignited growth in the plant and stirred up some hope within me. Just maybe it was possible that I could recover from my depression. Perhaps I could feel fully alive once again.

This little slip of green growth was a sprout of hope for me. It didn't cure my depression, but it made me believe a cure might be possible. I kept this plant image before me in the months ahead as I worked my way to wellness. In the process, I learned much about depression. I learned it can mean many things and take on many forms.

Depression can be feeling blue, being down in the dumps, or being extremely discouraged.

It can be something that's evident only to you or may be something others notice. They ask, "What's wrong?" You shrug your shoulders. You have no idea what they are talking about.

It can be a normal reaction to loss or stress, or it can feel completely abnormal—*where did this come from?*

It can be something that requires professional help or something you can work through without professional help.

Whatever form the depression takes, each gives you a feeling of hopelessness, and yet, truth be told, some little vestige of hope remains within you. It's encased in the hard soil of your situation, waiting to be resurrected. It needs some watering for a breakthrough to occur and to sustain itself. That's what this book is going to help us with. It's not going to cover everything there is to know about depression, but rather with Scripture, reflections, quotes, and stories, it will sprinkle water on the hardened soil that's choking the life out of you. With enough moisture, with some care and attention, hope can be activated. My hope is you'll begin to feel better about life, about yourself, and about God. I hope that you'll see possibilities where you thought none existed.

DAY 2

WHEN HOPE BECOMES HOPELESSNESS

The burdens . . . were so great and so heavy that we gave up all hope.

—2 CORINTHIANS 1:8

AFTER the slip of new green growth appeared, I regularly watered the fern. As I did, I couldn't help but wonder why the owner hadn't. Maybe she was so busy she didn't have time to consider the plant's needs. Or maybe the plant had been a gift, and she just didn't know what to do with it—she had never given plant care much thought.

I know I never gave much thought to hope until I became depressed. Hope simply operated in my life, moved me forward to the next challenge, and kept me feeling fully alive. While I often thought and talked about faith and love and worked at having those qualities in my life, I hadn't thought the same way about hope. I might have gone on like this forever if burdens hadn't started stacking up for me as they did for the Apostle Paul.

Near the beginning of his second letter to the Corinthians, Paul mentioned experiencing devastating hardships in Ephesus. He was "under great pressure, far beyond [his] ability to endure," so much so that he "despaired of life itself" (1:8 NIV). In his heart, he felt "the sentence of death" (v. 9 NIV), a symptom of severe depression.

No one knows for sure what happened in Ephesus to cause Paul to feel this way. It could have been the rioting against him after his successful teaching in the synagogue and in the secular hall of Tyrannus.

In an earlier letter to the Corinthians, Paul mentioned fighting beasts in Ephesus (see 1 Corinthians 15:32). It's unlikely he actually fought real beasts because he was a Roman citizen, and no Roman citizen could be made to do this. He may have been referring to people. You may know some beastly people!

It could be an accumulation of all those things because Paul said, "The burdens laid upon us were . . . great and . . . heavy" (2 Corinthians 1:8).

My stack of burdens started when my husband and I moved from a place I dearly loved to a place I didn't like. I went reluctantly, but I went because Bob and I believed God was calling him to an administrative position at a major Christian university. Before the first year was up, Bob was fired from this position. Unable to find another job in Christian higher education, a field saturated with applicants, he took a job at a Bible training center as an administrator and teacher. While the center wasn't accredited, we felt God's leading. He was fired from this job too.

Bob earnestly looked for a job in higher education. At the same time, he took a job at a window factory for minimum wage, trying to earn enough to buy gas and groceries for our family of five. I added babysitting to my self-employment income as a writer. We used Bob's severance pay to cover house payments and utilities.

Some jobs became available in the large church we attended. Bob had a seminary education, he was an administrator, and he loved to preach and teach, so perhaps God wanted him to go into ministry. Our pastor concurred. Bob didn't get those jobs either.

Now, here is where I added a layer to the stack that probably didn't need to be there. I started dwelling on the rejection. I also became irritated and resentful when members said, "God's got something better in mind for Bob," or, "When God closes a door, He always opens a window."

Unwanted moves, job losses (even if they are the spouse's job), financial struggles, disappointment in God's leadership, and rejection are the kinds of things that can cause people to become depressed. But so far I had not been depressed. While we had some discouraging days, I remained hopeful that God would eventually open up a position in which Bob could work as a Christian college administrator.

The day came, though, when the severance pay was depleted. We wouldn't be able to get by on minimum wage and babysitting money, so Bob found a job totally outside his field. He went to work as an executive recruiter, and I went to work trying to make sense of what happened. This is when I felt the weight of my burdens and "gave up all hope" (v. 8).

I don't know if I could tell you the exact moment hope became hopelessness. All I know is that I stopped wanting to get up in the morning, something very unusual for me, a morning person by nature. I felt there was no reason to go on with life. Nothing was ever going to change. It was during these bleak days that I began to understand how valuable hope is to the human spirit, how necessary it is to keep us moving forward and to feeling fully alive. If I wanted hope back, it was going to require the same attention and care I often gave faith and love. This was an insight that would help me the rest of my life.

WHAT COLOR IS HOPE?

*Blessed is the one who trusts in the L*ORD*, whose confidence is in him. They will be like a tree planted by the water that sends out its roots by the stream. It does not fear when heat comes; its leaves are always green.*

—JEREMIAH 17:7–8 NIV

H AVE you noticed how we use colors to describe feelings and actions?

She turned *white* as a sheet when she received the terrible news.

His face turned *red* as a beet when co-workers questioned his project proposal.

After five straight days of rain, her somber expression prompted someone to say to her, "You must be feeling *blue*."

Depressed people often describe their mood by saying, "I feel like I'm down in a *black* hole." Maybe you have said this.

I've read that *yellow* was once associated with jealousy, but now we refer to jealousy as "the *green*-eyed monster." A person who strongly wants what someone else has is said to be *green* with envy.

Linking green with jealousy and envy gives the color a negative vibe, but green is also used in a positive sense. For example, we say people or companies who cut back on electricity, fuel, or other things that damage the environment are "going *green*."

Personally, I associate hope with *green*. I'm sure that doesn't surprise you since you've already learned I can be moved by a little slip of green in a clay pot of hardened soil.

Green speaks to me of life and vitality. Something growing—whether inside my house or outside—nourishes my spirit, encourages more growth, and draws me to God. I don't know how writers live in high-rises where all they can see is concrete. I'd also struggle to work in a room full of cubicles. I need to see green. In my office, my desk is in front of a large window where I can look out on a green lawn and oak trees. Beside my desk is a luscious fern. Green blesses me so much that I think the streets of heaven should be lined with trees whose leaves are always green. Now that would be heaven to me!

What color would you associate with hope? Green? Blue? Purple? Red? There's not a right or wrong answer. By asking, I want to stir your thoughts about hope and raise your awareness of its power. Hope diminishes when we are depressed. We want and need our level of hope to rise if we want to recover and move forward in our lives.

The prophet Jeremiah often used word pictures, symbols, and poetic phrases to get people thinking about hope, as I'm using color. In one of his word pictures, he contrasted two types of plants—a shrub in a parched desert and a tree planted by the water.

When a person is experiencing hopelessness—what Jeremiah called the cursed life—he is "like a bush in the desert, which grows in the dry wasteland . . . Nothing good ever happens to him" (Jeremiah 17:6). In other words, this person has a dire existence.

In contrast to the cursed life is the blessed life, a life filled with hope. When a person experiences this, he is like a tree planted by water. The tree sends out roots taking in the water. "Its leaves are always green" (v. 8 NIV).

In reality, unless a tree is evergreen, its leaves aren't always green. The leaves of those oak trees in my front yard turn brown, wither, and eventually fall to the ground. But Jeremiah was using poetic language to draw a picture of a person who thrives. Leaves that are always green symbolize a life full of vitality, a life worth aiming for and sustaining. The person who has this kind of life "does not fear when heat comes," is not anxious when there's a "drought and never fails to bear fruit" (v. 8 NIV).

Now don't let this picture discourage you by making you think you could never sustain a life like that. Jeremiah didn't. Scripture seems to indicate he struggled with depression. He didn't always thrive in his role as a prophet. He knew times of intense loneliness and despair, times when he was a shrub living in a parched area, one that was dry and *brown*. At one point, he said to God, "Do you intend to disappoint me like a stream that goes dry in the summer?" (15:18).

With God's help, Jeremiah eventually worked his way through his battles with hopelessness, and he came out of them wanting others to know the value of hope. He wanted to encourage us when we feel like a small shrub, trying to hold onto life when the land around us is dry. Perhaps we can eventually grow into a tree whose leaves are green—if not a tree, then at least a luscious fern! This doesn't mean it will happen immediately, but wanting it to happen is a good place to start.

It is not necessary to associate hope with a color—or with a plant!—to get better. If green or another color doesn't register with you, that's not a problem. What's important is recognizing that hope is vital to the health of the human spirit. To recover, hope needs to be resurrected and activated in our lives. Asking, "What color is hope?" is one way to start the process. What's your answer?

THE "WHY" QUESTION

Why am I so depressed?

—Psalm 42:5 HCSB

W HEN you have a really bad cold, the kind where you have to keep reaching for tissue, do you think, *Now, where did I catch this?* Do you mentally retrace your steps? *Let's see, who was sneezing around me? Who had a runny nose?*

When you wake up with your right leg throbbing with pain, do you think about what you did the day before? Do you wonder what you might have done to cause it to ache the way it does? *Did I hit it against something?*

You may ask similar questions about the depression you are experiencing. Whether your depression is mild, severe, or somewhere in between, you may wonder why you feel the way you do. Like the composer of Psalms 42 and 43, you repeatedly ask, "Why am I so depressed?"

If the answer isn't readily obvious, you might try answering this question: What kind of stress have I experienced or am I experiencing?

Stress triggers depression. A divorce, a move, a job termination, a failure, a sudden drastic change in income, or losing your home would all be considered stressful for most people. But individuals experience stress in different ways. A situation that requires substantial readjustment for one person might be a slight inconvenience for someone else.

We don't always connect stress with depression because our depression may be a delayed response to the stressful event. By the time depression occurs, you may be so separated from the stressful event you don't connect the two. You conclude, "I don't have any reason to be depressed."

Another challenge in answering the why question is that our stress may have multiple facets—there's not a single identifiable cause but a combination of causes. This may have been the case with the psalmist.

The composer of Psalms 42 and 43 (originally the two formed a single composition) was one of a band of singers and musicians in Jerusalem. He remembered how he had "walked with many, leading the festive procession to the house of God, with joyful and thankful shouts" (Psalm 42:4 HCSB). But now, at the expression of this psalm, he is in exile, forced to live outside the city of Jerusalem. He missed the worship experiences he had there. He now has adversaries who "taunt [him], as if crushing [his] bones" (v. 10 HCSB). His stress includes loss, forced exile, adjusting to a new place, being ridiculed, and experiencing pain. He reacted by asking, "Why am I so depressed?" (vv. 5, 11; 43:5 HCSB).

This is a good question to ask. Hope building may begin with asking why. It did for the psalmist. By the time his lament ended, his hope had increased, believing God would redeem his situation (see 43:3–5). In his mind's eye, he could see himself praising God with the lyre once again (v. 4 HCSB). There is nothing to be gained by ignoring the why; rather, there is much to gain by asking and answering the question, *Why am I depressed?*

When we figure out what stress we are experiencing, we gain understanding and insight. We know why we feel the way we do, and this helps stop the awful worry of wondering what terrible thing is wrong with us or what we might have done to deserve such misery.

Knowing why can reveal changes we might need to make in our lives to have better mental and spiritual health.

Knowing why can help determine a remedy or a treatment program.

Knowing why helps evaluate the severity of the problem. *Is this something I'm going to need help with to resolve? Is the stress going to take a long time to recover from, or is this something I can anticipate clearing up in a few months?*

Knowing why might also help expose some unhealthy roots in our lives that keep us from flourishing. Our depression may be alerting us to their presence and letting us know we might want to do something about them in the future. Even if we do nothing, at least we will know where some of our vulnerability to depression is coming from, and that can help us accept who we are.

Asking why is also beneficial because it releases some of the exasperation boiling inside us. Not only does this provide some relief, but it also keeps us from transferring our negative feelings to God or blaming someone we live or work with.

But what if we can't answer why? What if we can't determine the reason for our depression? It could mean we need the help of mental health or medical professionals. The fog of our depression keeps us from thinking clearly and reaching conclusions; therefore, we may need guidance and skill to find the answer.

Even if we don't discover the answer now, someday we may figure it out. Then we'll be able to look back at our lives with a "now I get it" understanding. Until that happens, we can rest assured we are not crazy, odd, or weird. We are having a reaction to stress of some kind.

What we don't want to do is to keep asking why or think we can't get better unless we know why. That's simply not true. Knowing why is very helpful but not absolutely necessary, because there's a better question to ask. That question begins with "what" as in, "Now that I'm depressed, *what* I am going to do about it?"

DAY 5

FROM FULL TO EMPTY

I went away full, but the LORD has brought me back empty.

—RUTH 1:21 NIV

SOMETIMES when we're trying to answer a question, we need it said another way in order to respond. To determine why you are depressed, I suggested asking, *What stress am I experiencing or have experienced?* Another question that has worked equally well for me is, *What have I lost?* Depression is often a response to loss.

The loss could be what I call a tangible one. Your house burns down. A loved one dies. A divorce occurs. A job is lost. The plant—where you've worked for 20 years—closes. Even something like the loss of pictures and scrapbooks can cause depression.

The loss could also be intangible, something that others don't see but is vital to your mental and spiritual health.

The dreams you had as a young adult that never materialized.

The belief you've held that goodness is rewarded but now doesn't seem to be true.

The disappointment you feel in your life. You often find yourself wondering, *Is this all there is?*

Naomi is a person who experienced both tangible and intangibles losses.

Naomi had a life filled with family, friends, faith, and familiarity, and then a famine forced her, her husband, and their sons to leave their home in Bethlehem and move to the land of Moab. The Moabites disliked Israelites, so they weren't met with open arms; nevertheless, they made the best of their new situation. Naomi's sons married Moabite women (Orpah and Ruth), and she looked forward to having grandchildren someday. Then her husband died, and one by one, her sons died. Her many losses left her feeling bereft.

Similarly, my life had once been "full." Before we moved, my husband was a college administrator. We lived in a house I liked, one I never wanted to leave. We had just had our third son. We loved and were active in our church. And then we moved to a "foreign land"! Our move wasn't prompted by a famine. We were conscientious Christians trying our best to do what we perceived as God's will—a new job in a new state.

From the time we arrived, the adjustment did not go well. As you know, Bob lost this job, found another, and then lost it. Along with these job difficulties came a big reduction in income. The neighborhood and yard didn't suit our active family. We lost the regard of fellow church members at the church we attended. At least, I perceived it that way.

While these are the kinds of stressors that can cause depression, I had not been depressed during the move, the job losses, or the rejection.

It was when our lives gave the *appearance* of stabilizing that I became depressed. In other words, to people around us, our lives looked fine. Bob had a job—not in his field, but one that would pay the bills. The days of, "What will we eat?" and, "How will we pay our bills?" were over. We had moved to the country, where our boys could be as active as they wanted without disturbing anyone. We had changed churches, so we were no longer at the one where we experienced rejection.

About this time, I started experiencing lower back pain. I found it hard to move, as if my feet were embedded in concrete. I kept reaching inside for strength to cope, but nothing was there. A morning person by nature, I no longer wanted to get out of bed.

I was certain something terrible was wrong. I went to the doctor, and he concluded, "You are depressed." He encouraged me to see a psychiatrist, which I did. Through several sessions with him and with effort on my part, I got better. The physical symptoms ceased, and I could move easier. But inwardly I identified with Naomi.

Not knowing how to manage without sons or a husband, Naomi returned home to Bethlehem. When she arrived, the stark contrast of what her life used to be and what it was now flooded her mind. She said to her friends, "I went away full, but the LORD has brought me back empty" (Ruth 1:21 NIV).

I recognized her feelings of emptiness because I felt the same way, even though I couldn't put it into words. I still have a hard time describing it. There was nothing in my inner space on which I could draw for energy or support. If I reached my hand down inside to get some emotional resolve or inner strength, there was nothing to pull out. No hope. No security. No joy. No vitality.

But once I was diagnosed, I started reading about depression. I learned loss and depression are often linked. I had experienced many obvious losses, but it seemed none of those were causing my emptiness, so I asked myself, *What have I really lost?*

Through much prayer and reflection, I eventually realized what I had lost. At every step, my husband and I had sincerely sought God's will and followed it with trusting hearts. When I added up all that happened, it didn't make sense. Since it didn't, I concluded that God did not have a purpose for our lives. That intangible but very important *belief* had always been there. Now it was gone. The result was depleted of something necessary to vibrant living.

Knowing what I lost—my belief that God has a purpose for our lives—didn't mean, though, that I could simply zap the belief back into my heart, instantly refilling the hole. But answering the question helped me realize what was wrong. Now I had to answer the more important question, *What was I going to do about it?*

DAY 6

WILL IT EVER END?

The path you walk may be dark indeed.

—Isaiah 50:10

S TRESSFUL events—the kinds that trigger depression—
can often be linked to a specific time: the night we broke
up, the day my father died, the day the factory closed. Not
that your depression started at that exact moment! Rather the
event serves as a point of reference for you. When your doctor
asks, "When did you start feeling so hopeless?" or, "When did
your sleeplessness start?" you might say something like, "Ever
since our house flooded, and we lost so many possessions."

Another stress-related trigger is chronic stress. This
kind of stress is ongoing. Day after day you have to deal with
a particularly hard situation. You weren't depressed when the
situation began, but somewhere in the process of dealing with
it, your mood started changing. You find yourself being more
pessimistic, your energy diminishing, your sleep being
disturbed, and your appetite changing. You can't pinpoint the
exact moment the depression began, but it happened when
dealing with a tension-filled situation.

Your teenage child defies every rule you set, questions
every statement you make. He is sullen and unpredictable. You
wonder what happened to that compliant, pleasant child you
once had.

Your grown child moves in with you, bringing two
children along. At first, you were glad to help out, but you
thought it would be temporary. As the stay extends, your
patience as a grandmother wears thin. You find yourself
longing for solitude.

You don't have enough income to cover all your
expenses. You're constantly juggling bills, trying to stay afloat.
People say money can't buy happiness, but the lack of it sure
looks like it is buying depression for you.

When you father had a stroke, you took him in after
his medical benefit payments for rehabilitation ran out. You

wanted to do it; your intentions were the best, but you never realized how exhausting caring for him would be. As the days wear on, you resent being so confined, and you feel guilty for being resentful!

You follow your boss's instructions only to have him change his mind. And his standards? They are so exacting. He's impossible to please, and yet you keep trying because you don't want to lose your job. You would never find another that pays as well.

Some people manage chronic stress without becoming depressed, but others don't. The continual tension erodes strength. Every morning, the same challenge is present, booming, pervading, and demanding. *Will it ever end?* An ending may come—that rebellious teen will grow up!—but the problem is, there's no end in sight.

Without a resolution, hopelessness starts subtly making itself at home in your heart. The brightness of life fades. You feel like you are walking in darkness even though you "honor the Lord and obey the words of his servant" (Isaiah 50:10).

Gary and Penny experienced this darkness after Gary became Penny's caregiver. He resigned his salaried position so they could move across country to get medical treatment for Penny. The particular surgeon they needed for her brain surgery was on the East Coast. Their hopes were high as they embarked, but they were dashed when the surgery did not achieve what the doctors had predicted. In addition, Penny suffered much discomfort after the surgery.

Gary took a nine-to-five hourly job to help them get by financially. It was a simple, undemanding job that allowed him to be emotionally available for Penny as well as take care of her physical needs. At the end of every workday, Gary would come home to their apartment to find Penny no better. He said, "Darkness fell long before nightfall."

As days turned into weeks, and weeks into months, Gary wondered, *Will Penny ever fully recover? Will life return to what it once was?* Separated from family and friends, they also began feeling separated from God. Gary felt so alone, unable to make contact with God. He was too weary to articulate his prayers as he once had.

One night as Gary lay in bed unable to sleep, he reached his arms into the air. He couldn't see his arms in the darkness. It didn't matter; they were raised. He wanted to reach out and touch God somehow.

He persisted in reaching out in the darkness, night after night, touching nothing and feeling nothing. In his own way, raising his arms, penetrating the darkness, became Gary's prayer. He was asking, *God, are You there?*

It is important during these times when we don't feel God's presence to not abandon the beliefs we hold dear. As Isaiah says, "the path you walk may be dark indeed, but trust in the LORD, rely on your God" (v. 10). Our time of darkness is a time to keep trusting, even if it is with a small gesture like Gary's. This gesture showed he still believed God was real and that he trusted Him.

Gradually, Penny's health returned, and Gary returned to the kind of work he used to do. One night as he lay in bed thinking back over their season of trial, he realized God hadn't abandoned them. He had been with them all the time. There were no fireworks, no light shows, just that simple reassurance that those who walk in faith know. Their path was no longer dark; they were back walking in the light.

DAY 7

THE LAST STRAW

*I can't be responsible for all these people
by myself; it's too much.*

—NUMBERS 11:14

WHEN I think of Moses, I always see a Charlton Heston type—tall, strong, and forceful. I'm sure this comes from having watched *The Ten Commandments*. I see Moses as a man who can masterfully handle whatever comes his way. In the movie, he's always in command of himself and others, yet the Bible shows this powerful man becoming frustrated with his many responsibilities.

God called Moses to lead more than 600,000 Israelite men plus women, children, sheep, goats, and cattle from Egypt to the Promised Land (see Exodus 12:37–38). A job this size would depress me! Not Moses, though. He wasn't daunted.

Through a series of plagues, Moses (through God's power) gained the Israelite's release from the Egyptian pharaoh, and the Israelites headed for the Promised Land. Then Pharaoh changed his mind. He ordered his army to pursue the Israelites and bring them back to Egypt. When the Israelites saw Pharaoh's army coming after them, they were terrified. Moses, strong man of faith that he was, said, "Do not be afraid. Stand firm and you will see the deliverance the LORD will bring to you today" (Exodus 14:13 NIV). And they did! The Red Sea parted before them, allowing them to escape the pursuing Egyptians.

With such a dramatic rescue, you would think the Israelites would be forever grateful to God and would willingly follow His servant Moses. Instead they protested and whined. They worried about having water to drink and meat to eat. They accused Moses of bringing them into the wilderness to starve them to death. The people worshiped idols when Moses made it clear that God commanded them not to. At one point, God became impatient with their behavior. He sent fire among them, which ceased only after Moses pleaded with God on their behalf (see Numbers 11:1–3).

Moses held on through all of these frustrating circumstances and more. He interceded on behalf of the people and trusted God to help them, and He did. God provided water to drink and manna to eat.

While Moses grew angry at times, he was faithful to the task. It was a "last straw" that drove him to despair.

The Israelites were tired of the daily supply of manna. They wanted chewy meat, crunchy vegetables, spicy foods, and fish like they had in Egypt. They said, "There is nothing at all to eat—nothing but this manna day after day!" (v. 6).

Forgetting what their lives were like in Egypt, the people wept and complained within earshot of Moses. God heard them, too, and He "became exceedingly angry" (v. 10 NIV). Now Moses was caught between a complaining people and an angry God. This was too much!

> *And he said to the LORD, "Why have you treated me so badly? Why are you displeased with me? Why have you given me the responsibility for all these people? I didn't create them or bring them to birth! Why should you ask me to act like a nurse and carry them in my arms like babies all the way to the land you promised to their ancestors? . . . I can't be responsible for all these people by myself; it's too much for me! If you are going to treat me like this, have pity on me and kill me, so that I won't have to endure your cruelty any longer." —vv. 11–15*

It's in this honest prayer that I see signs of Moses's depression.

He prayed to die. Wanting to die is a symptom of severe depression.

He felt sorry for himself. Depressive episodes are often filled with self-pity.

He saw the situation as impossible. Moses felt hopeless even though he had experienced God's miraculous interventions all along the journey from Egypt.

He felt worthless, as if he had failed at everything.

That is how I see it with my twenty-first-century eyes, but anyone on the scene who didn't have the whole picture might think something like this: *Can you believe Moses got so upset by people wanting leeks and onions that he lost his cool? Isn't he overreacting?*

What they were observing, though, wasn't a one-time incident. It was the last straw on top of a pile of straws. When we say, "it's the straw that breaks the camel's back," we mean it's the last in a series of annoyances and disappointments that leads to a final loss of patience, temper, trust, or hope. But that last straw couldn't have the effect it does if the other straws hadn't already been in place.

Some of us may arrive at places like this where our stack of responsibilities and concerns become too heavy, and we feel as "wretched" as Moses did (v. 15 KJV). When the last straw lands, our eruption may be a very honest prayer like Moses's or it may mean turning in your resignation or telling your siblings they are not treating you fairly.

If Paul is right about our being "common clay pots" (2 Corinthians 4:7), then all of us are capable of having a breaking point and becoming depressed. Not everyone will, but if we do, we are in good company. Lots of strong people have experienced depression. In addition to Moses, there's Buzz Aldrin, Irving Berlin, Carol Burnett, Johnny Carson, Winston Churchill, and Emily Dickinson, to name a few.

Whether their depression was caused by too many responsibilities, I don't know. I do know this: they went on to live notable lives, and that possibility is there for us too. The very strengths that enable us to take on responsibilities will also help us recover—though it might take getting rid of a few of those straws we're carrying on our backs. Depression is not a sign of weakness as much as it is a sign of weariness.

DAY 8

WHAT AM I FEELING?

When hope is crushed, the heart is crushed.

—PROVERBS 13:12

WE SHOULDN'T talk about stressful events, loss, chronic stress, and overwhelming responsibilities without also mentioning feelings and emotions that are intertwined with the stress we experience.

Job grieved after his catastrophic losses. When his friends came to be with him, "they saw that his grief was very great" (Job 2:13 KJV). Job himself said, "My grief has almost made me blind; my arms and legs are as thin as shadows" (17:7). In other words he had a hard time focusing, and he was losing weight—both symptoms of depression.

Jonah asked God to end his life rather than send him to preach repentance to the people of Nineveh (Jonah 4:3). He didn't like it when God showed them mercy. He "became angry" (v. 1) and petulant.

King Saul's anger, anxiety, jealousy, sorrow, fear, guilt, suspicion, and insecurity could have all contributed to depression, keeping it alive and growing.

Cynicism may have gotten the best of King Solomon when life didn't turn out the way he thought it should. He wrote, "We labor, trying to catch the wind, and what do we get? We get to live our lives in darkness and grief, worried, angry, and sick" (Ecclesiastes 5:16–17).

The stressful things that trigger our depression—whether an event, a loss, a chronic situation, overwhelming responsibilities, or something else—are like seeds planted in our inner space—the place we often refer to as the *heart*. These stressors come with feelings—feelings that get stored in our inner space. If these feelings aren't expressed, dealt with, or acknowledged, their presence can act as powerful fertilizer for the seed of depression, causing it to sprout, grow, and thrive.

I once read an article in *People* magazine about the artist Elizabeth Layton (a.k.a. Grandma Layton). She never realized the impact her emotions had on her unhappiness until she experienced relief at age 68. When Elizabeth married at 19, she and her husband moved away from her hometown of Wellsville, Kansas. The marriage didn't go well. After a series of separations, she went back to Wellsville, ran her family's newspaper, got a divorce, and raised five children, all while dealing with depression.

After her divorce, Elizabeth started having severe headaches along with her chronic depression. She underwent 13 shock treatments when the pain became unbearable. With the relief she experienced, she felt more hopeful about the future and married businessman Glenn Layton. Still, the depression hung on. Even with psychotherapy and antidepressant drug treatment, Elizabeth continued to battle depression, even hiding in her closet.

She felt unworthy of life, and when her son died, she hit bottom. Her depression might have gone on forever if her sister hadn't urged her to take an art class. She thought it might cheer her up. Elizabeth was skeptical; nevertheless, she went.

The art class was in contour drawing, a technique in which the artist looks at the subject while drawing and only occasionally glancing at the art they are creating. This practice allows the artist to focus on the subject rather than what they are creating.

Elizabeth chose herself as the subject, which meant she had to look at herself in a mirror while she drew her portrait. She depicted herself as an old hag, but—and here's what's important—once she finished, she couldn't stop. She said, "I don't know where it came from, but I had this sense of urgency to keep drawing." As she continued drawing self-portraits, Elizabeth was able to release long-suppressed emotions. Drawing her feelings enabled her to become free of the deep bouts of depression that had plagued her for 40 years.

In the process, her depression was exorcised. The contour drawing exercises transformed her life. She simply didn't feel depressed any more.

At first she when she started drawing herself, she saw herself as ugly, as "a sagging mass of spotted flesh around sad eyes." As her depression gradually lifted, "she began to draw herself as a confident, lively woman." Within a year, she saw "a more serene face in her mirror." Hopelessness was replaced with hopefulness.

Her art therapy resulted in wonderful works of art that were first exhibited in Kansas and later throughout the United States. Shortly before she died, her works were the focus of shows at the Smithsonian's National Museum of American Art and the Delaware Art Musuem. But the honors she received are not why her story is mentioned here. It is here to remind all of us of the importance of releasing emotions—whether through art or in another way that better fits our personality— that contribute to our depression and keep us from being hopeful people. Unexpressed emotions fill our hearts, taking up valuable inner space—space hope needs to thrive. That's why we want to watch over our hearts "with all diligence; for from it flow the springs of life" (Proverbs 4:23 RSV). We don't want fertile soil for growing depression; we want fertile soil for growing hope.

WHEN GOD'S TO BLAME

The LORD's hand has turned against me!

—RUTH 1:13 NIV

WHILE we link depression with stress and emotions, we need to also mention spiritual connections. This is getting complicated, isn't it? Well, depression is complicated because it can include physical, mental, social, emotional, and spiritual components. That's why I said from the beginning this book would not cover everything there is to know about depression!

Rather this book is about hope, a quality so important to the human spirit. Hope keeps us moving forward in life, believing good things are possible and that we have some power to make it so. In depression, hope shrivels. To keep hope alive and active, we need to understand that spiritual issues, particularly our relationship with God, may be involved. We may even think our depression is His fault.

The psalmist who asked, "Why am I depressed?" was a strong believer who thirsted after God and who had phenomenal worship experiences (Psalm 42:5). God was his Rock, yet in his depression, he said to God, "Why have you forgotten me?" (v. 9 NIV).

When Moses's "last straw" landed, he cried out, "Why have *you* treated me so badly? Why are *you* displeased with me?" (Numbers 11:11, author's emphasis).

When Naomi returned to Bethlehem, her former home, she said to her old friends, "Call me Marah" (Ruth 1:20), which means bitter. Her name, Naomi, the one her friends knew her by, meant pleasant. The new name indicated a change in Naomi—a negative change "because Almighty God has made [her] life bitter" (v. 20). He had "condemned [her] and sent [her] trouble" (v. 21).

Job's many losses didn't jive with his and his friends' traditional beliefs. If you sin, you suffer. If you repent, the suffering stops. Job's friends were certain he must have sinned to have such terrible things happen to him. Job insisted he did nothing wrong and would continue to trust in the Lord even if God killed him. Still, it would mean so much to him if he just knew what God's complaints against him were. Didn't God owe him an explanation?

> *I always expected to live a long life and to die at home in comfort. I was like a tree whose roots always have water and whose branches are wet with dew.*
>
> —Job 29:18–19

> *Now I am about to die; there is no relief for my suffering. . . . God seizes me by my collar . . . throws me down in the mud . . . I call to you, O God, but you never answer; and when I pray, you pay no attention.*
>
> —30:16–20

Job's friends found his reaction hard to understand, and people may find it hard to empathize with us when our depression involves spiritual issues. No one seemed to understand what a loss it was for me to no longer believe God had a purpose for our lives. Even if I just hinted at it, people would say, "Oh Brenda, of course God has a purpose for your life." That would silence me, and I would say no more, thus lengthening my depression.

If you asked Susie why she was depressed, she would say, "A phone call that never came."

You might say, "What?! How could you say that when people are losing their homes and jobs? Now *those* are reasons for being depressed!" But Susie had experienced loss; she lost an intangible—the belief that caring among Christians is reciprocated.

Susie was an active church member, a "dream" church member, really. She was an enthusiastic volunteer, always ready to help with the next project. She had the kind of personality that would take in everyone in a group and cause the members to mesh. At her own initiative, she organized and led groups for the bereaved. She was "there" for them.

When her husband died unexpectedly, no one from the church checked on her in the days after the funeral. No one came by to see how she was doing. In the bereavement group she led, she actually said, "I need someone to call me." Still, no one did, and she was profoundly disappointed. In all her service to others, she thought she was pleasing God and He would bless her for it. She always believed what she did for others would be returned to her if she ever needed it. But when the time came, no one came forward, and the whole faith thing seemed like a sham. *Why doesn't God, the God I faithfully served, prompt someone to call me?*

Andrew Solomon, in his atlas on depression, *The Noonday Demon*, says that for many people, depression is "an experience of being cast out by God or abandoned by Him." He says for most believers, "this rage against God lifts as the depression does." In time, as we work our way out of hopelessness, our rage does lift as we remember God never leaves or forsakes us (Deuteronomy 31:6; Joshua 1:5; Hebrews 13:5). This is true even when we feel otherwise. Facts and feelings aren't always the same. When the period of depression ends, you'll discover, as I did, that He was there all the time.

THE THIRST
OF DEPRESSION

*As the deer pants for streams of water, so
my soul pants for you, my God.*

—Psalm 42:1 NIV

D o you feel as though you are being drowned by your circumstances? Sometimes depressed people feel this way. Sorrows or troubles seem to come in waves, and you fear you will collapse under the deluge. This is the way the psalmist, the one who asked, "Why am I so depressed?" may have felt. He said to God, "In the roar of your waterfalls; all your waves and breakers have swept over me" (Psalm 42:7 NIV).

As he listened to the roar of the waterfall, watching wave after wave crash on the rocks below, he was struck by its power. He wondered if anyone could survive underneath the cascade. Simultaneously, he wondered if he would survive the "waves" that were overwhelming him.

What were some of those waves?

He wasn't in Jerusalem any more; he was in exile. While we do not know his exact location or how he got there, he is clear about it being against his will. It was "breaking" his heart (v. 6).

He could no longer worship God at the Temple in Jerusalem. In his way of thinking, this meant he could no longer experience God as he once did, for God's people at that time associated God's presence with the Temple. He added to this wave something some depressed people often do. He attached the word *never*. He assumed he would *never* experience God like he once did. His hopelessness didn't allow for any sense of possibility.

Not being at the Temple meant he could not participate in dynamic worship, and he missed leading and participating in worship with his relatives. Before, they "went with the crowds to the house of God and led them as they walked along, a happy crowd, singing and shouting praise to God" (v. 4).

Now he was tormented and taunted by enemies (see vv. 9 and 43:2*b*). Who these enemies were, we don't know. They could have been the people who forced him into exile, or it could have been those people who got tired of him talking about "the good ole days" in Jerusalem. Whatever the reason, the psalmist was weary of being mistreated.

Perhaps the worst wave of all was feeling abandoned by God. God had been his Rock, his stronghold, so why wasn't God rescuing him? Why had God rejected him when he needed Him so? His yearning for God was so strong that he likened it to an out-of-breath, panting deer that had been running hard and was thirsty for streams of water.

The psalmist was a strong believer whose faith was challenged by his circumstances. His faith, though, while shaken enough to cause him to be depressed, also helped him get well.

Like many other psalmists, this man earnestly sought God by lamenting. In other words, he complained. He told God exactly how he felt. The psalmist's restoration began with admitting his feelings to God.

The beginning of our recovery may start at the same place. Lamenting isn't the only way to release feelings, but admitting them to God is a safe place to do it. It's safe in the sense that God will not tell. Some of us may be reluctant to tell anyone what "waves" we are dealing with. The waves may be petty issues, or, at least, we believe they would appear petty to others. They are major issues in our eyes. Some of us are depressed because of things we have done wrong. Unresolved guilt haunts us, and yet we are terrified with the prospect of anyone finding out. These are the things we can take to God when we are concerned no one will understand or when someone else might be shocked.

For our laments to be effective, we need to describe what we are feeling as the psalmist did. In our prayers, many of us do not spend much time describing our problems along with the associated feelings. We may be more likely to pray, "Oh God, help me to start feeling better," or, "Dear God, be with me," over and over again. However, it can be very beneficial to honestly describe how we feel. It was for the psalmist.

Once he expressed his anger and resentment, his sense of feeling far away from God began to fade. His confidence began to return. He asked God to vindicate him and to defend him (43:1). He believed God could and would do something about his situation.

Of course, the psalmist's confidence wavered again, and this may happen to us. It's the nature of depression that when we're trying hard to pull ourselves out of darkness, it draws us back in. The psalmist, though, didn't let the darkness win. He continued. He questioned God about rejecting him. With this honesty, a positive shift took place.

He said to God, "Send me your light and your faithful care, let them lead me; let them bring me to your holy mountain, to the place where you dwell" (v. 3 NIV). He referred to God as his "joy" and "delight" and pledged to praise God "with the lyre" (v. 4 NIV). He then encouraged others by saying, "put your hope in God" (v. 5 NIV).

What occurred was not a geographical shift; the psalmist was not immediately transported back to Jerusalem, to the Temple, to the way things were. Rather, a spiritual victory occurred, giving him hope for the future.

The psalmist's lament bears testimony not to the weakness of his faith but to its strength. He poured out his heart to God, admitted his feelings, and, in so doing, regained hope. His depressive thirst was satisfied, and ours can be too. Recovery is possible because "God, who comforts the depressed" (2 Corinthians 7:6 NASB), will comfort us.

DAY 11

THE VALUE OF
HONEST PRAYING

My God, my God, why hast thou forsaken me?
—MARK 15:34 KJV

WHEN you've been working in the yard, running a race, or moving heavy furniture, what do you reach for? You reach for water, don't you? Now if we think of spiritually alleviating our thirst, how might we reach out for living water?

The psalmist whose soul panted for God showed us how he reached for a drink by lamenting. He acknowledged his feelings, and in so doing gave God a "cup" in which God could respond to him. Other people in the Bible who exhibited symptoms of being depressed also held out their "cups" through honest praying. They expressed their thoughts and emotions to God, even to the point of wanting to die.

After the exciting but strenuous duel with the Baal prophets on Mount Carmel and Jezebel's subsequent threat on his life, Elijah ran away to the wilderness. Disappointed and miserable, Elijah cried out to God, "I've had enough . . . Take away my life. I've got to die sometime, and it might as well be now" (1 Kings 19:4 TLB).

Moses, as you recall from Day 7, questioned God calling him. "Why have you given me the responsibility for all these people? . . . If you are going to treat me like this, have pity on me and kill me, so that I won't have to endure your cruelty any longer" (Numbers 11:11–15).

Likewise, Jeremiah questioned God about the fairness of life. "Why do dishonest people succeed? You plant them, and they take root; they grow and bear fruit. They always speak well of you, yet they do not really care about you" (Jeremiah 12:1–2). He was angered by the perceived unfairness and wanted to get rid of those who caused it. His honest prayer makes me wince as he says to God, "Drag these evil people away like sheep to be butchered; guard them until it is time for them to be slaughtered" (v. 3).

Jonah was greatly displeased and became angry when God mercifully forgave the repentant citizens of Nineveh. He explained why he ran away from God in his prayer: "I knew that you are a gracious and compassionate God, slow to anger and abounding in love, a God who relents from sending calamity. Now, LORD, take away my life, for it is better for me to die than to live" (Jonah 4:2–3 NIV).

I was unfamiliar with these prayers when I was depressed—unfamiliar in the sense that I didn't see them as tools for fighting depression. I had read these incidents of prayer many times, but I didn't make the connection that I might need to do something similar sometime. I was, though, a student of Jesus' prayer life. Without realizing it, one of His prayers—a very honest one—was indelibly printed on my soul: His cry expressing His feelings of abandonment as He hung on the Cross. When I needed to reach for a drink of thirst-satisfying water, it was there for me to use.

Depression is a tenacious foe—it wants to stick around, hang on, and find a good home. I made great strides in getting well after my diagnosis. The visits with the psychiatrist had ended. The physical symptoms were gone. I was back to being an early riser and tackling the responsibilities of my day, but little things would happen that would trigger hurtful memories. By four o'clock in the afternoon, I could feel the darkness of depression coming back.

One day as I was peeling potatoes, preparing our family's supper, I thought, *I can't stand this any longer.* I ran to the bathroom (the only room in the house with a lock on the door) and knelt on the floor. With tears flowing, I prayed my version of Jesus' desperate prayer from the Cross: "My God, my God, why have you forsaken me?" (Mark 15:34 NIV).

"God," I prayed, "How could You do this to us? How could You hurt us when we tried so hard to serve You? How could You abandon us?" I said everything I felt until the emotion was spent. Then something clicked inside me, and suddenly God didn't seem so far away. Strengthened, I rose, washed my face, opened the door, and went back to preparing supper, free of the feelings that drove me to pray.

The next afternoon around four, the feelings were back. Without hesitating, I went to the bathroom, locked the door, and prayed the same way as the day before. This time wasn't as intense and didn't last as long. I repeated the same pattern for several days until the four o'clock blues stopped arriving.

I was surprised by the strong emotions that tumbled out during those bathroom prayertimes. Few people I know would be able to handle such raw emotion, but God can. We may shock our friends, but we cannot shock God. That's why we want to make sure we hold out our "cup" to God. We want the relief that comes from sharing our feelings, and we want to give God a channel for Him to respond and do a work of grace in our lives.

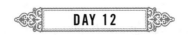

DAY 12

INSIGHTFUL
QUESTIONING

Now stand up straight and answer the questions I ask you.

—JOB 38:3

B ESIDES responding to honest praying, another way the Bible shows God helping those with signs of depression was through asking questions.

Elijah, on the run from Queen Jezebel, went into a cave to spend the night. The darkness of the cave closed in around him. He was disappointed and felt sorry for himself. Why go on? Why try so hard when it didn't seem to matter? Other people didn't care, why should he? This is when God asked him a very simple question. He said, "Elijah, what are you doing here?" (1 Kings 19:9, 13).

When God didn't punish the people of Nineveh, Jonah was furious. He was angry enough that he wanted to die. God asked him, "What right do you have to be angry?" (Jonah 4:4).

God asked Job numerous questions (see Job 38:2–41:34). For a time, God patiently allowed Job and his friends to discuss the reason Job experienced so many calamities, and then God responded.

> *Now stand up straight and answer the questions I ask you.*
> —38:3

> *Where were you when I laid the earth's foundation?*
> —v. 4 NIV

> *Who waters the dry and thirsty land, so that grass springs up?*
> —v. 27

> *Do you know when mountain goats are born?*
> —39:1

Question after question was directed to Job, including this zinger:

*Are you trying to prove that I am unjust—to put me
in the wrong and yourself in the right? Are you as strong
as I am?*

—40:8–9

Questions encourage us to think, to use our mental wheels.
Many who deal with depression experience sluggishness of the
mind. This can be a symptom of the depression itself, or it can
be a side effect of the medication individuals may be prescribed
to reduce depression symptoms. The mental gymnastics of
asking—and answering—questions improve our alertness, and
they can also add insight that might assist in recovery.

When God asked Elijah, "What are you doing here?"
He didn't mean, "Tell me your geographical location." He
meant, "How did you arrive at this point, hiding out in a cave
and feeling sorry for yourself?" If Elijah could answer this
question, he might be able to learn from his experience.

I realize, though, that "What are you doing here?" is
not an easy question to answer. God had to ask Elijah twice.
We may have to ask ourselves several times and mull the
question over for a time because depression, by its very nature,
is obstinate in its opposition to being investigated.

In Elijah's case, answering God's question gave him the
opportunity to vent and release his emotions. He said:

*Lord God Almighty, I have always served you—you
alone. But the people of Israel have broken their covenant
with you, torn down your altars, and killed all your
prophets. I am the only one left—and they are trying to
kill me!*

—1 Kings 19:10

As Elijah answered, it cleared out some of his inner space so he
could be ready for a spiritual lesson and to serve God again

(see vv. 11–12). God still purposed for Elijah to be an active prophet once again.

Answering God's question to Jonah also cleared inner space. God had been merciful to Jonah, rescuing him from the belly of a whale, just as he had been merciful to the Ninevites by not destroying them. God asked him, "What right do you have to be angry?" God didn't mean a person should never be angry. God wanted Jonah to look at himself, his pride, his lack of compassion, and his unwillingness to do what God wanted him to do.

God's question to Jonah reminds me to take stock of what I'm feeling when the dark clouds of depression start hovering. I ask myself, "What am I *really* feeling?" Sometimes I've been surprised to learn I'm jealous or envious. That's when I ask, "What right do I have to feel this way?" In a broad sense, I have a "right" as we all have a right to how we feel, but from God's perspective my jealousy and envy show I don't always have an appreciation for what He has called me to do. Once I gain this insight, I begin to take appropriate steps to keep the feelings from spiraling into depression.

As God questioned Job, he began to grasp something bigger than what he could see was going on, and there was. Those of us who've read the Book of Job know what was going on behind the scenes (see Job 1:1–2:6), but Job didn't know.

The possibility of another perspective is something we may want to consider in understanding why we feel the way we do. It could be we haven't considered the viewpoint of those we live with, work with, go to church with, or who've wronged us. Perhaps we haven't even considered God's perspective. And who knows, if we did, we may have a breakthrough as startling as Job's. He said, "In the past I knew only what others had told me, but now I have seen you with my own eyes" (Job 42:5). A result like that makes asking and answering questions worthwhile!

DAY 13

THE MOST IMPORTANT QUESTION

Do you want to get well?

—John 5:6 NIV

A MONG the many questions we might ask ourselves, the most important one may be the one Jesus asked when He was in Jerusalem for a religious festival. Near one of the city gates was a pool where a large crowd of sick people gathered—"the blind, the lame, and the paralyzed" (John 5:3). They gathered at the pool because they believed an angel stirred the water from time to time. They believed the first one to get into the pool after the water was stirred was healed from whatever disease he had. Among the sick was a man who had been ill for 38 years. "Jesus saw him lying there, and he knew that the man had been sick for such a long time; so he asked him, 'Do you want to get well?'" (v. 6).

Don't you find that a strange question? Why wouldn't anyone who had been sick for such a long time want to get well? Why would Jesus ask such a question?

The sick man told Jesus, "Sir, I don't have anyone here to put me in the pool when the water is stirred up; while I am trying to get in, somebody else gets there first" (v. 7). Was there nobody in the crowded city of Jerusalem who could help him get in the water? Had he thought of moving his mat close to the edge of the pool so he could quickly roll himself into the water?

Or perhaps Jesus' question had nothing to do with the man's past. Perhaps He was attempting to ignite the man's desire in order to get him ready for his future. If recovered, the man would have to take up life again with all its challenges, starting with picking up his mat and walking. There would be much to relearn; he would have to face many life responsibilities. Would he be determined enough to handle all of those?

This idea of the man needing to ignite his desire is what makes me believe Jesus' question is an important one to ask ourselves.

For some people, given time, depression will lift on its own. But for others of us, recovery is not a matter of time, it is a matter of work—work that requires motivation. Here are some reasons why.

Many who are depressed have to combat the inertia that plagues them. Their whole bodies are telling them to sit still—it just requires too much effort to move. The inertia could be part of the illness itself or it could be a side effect to certain antidepressants.

We believe there's nothing we can do. But that's just not true. There's never been a time when there's been more help available than there is now: biblical guidelines, self-help tools, therapies, exercises, medications, etc. The problem for some of us isn't that no help is available, but rather we are reluctant to access help. We think, *That tool may have worked for others, but it won't work for me. My case is different. My case is unique.*

Many of the available tools don't offer an instantaneous solution. For example, taking an antidepressant may take weeks to start being effective; it is not like taking an antibiotic for strep throat and seeing an immediate change. When we don't make progress right away, we're tempted to quit because we don't have the patience or confidence to keep trying.

No one tool works for everyone. For example, there's no one medication, no one exercise, or no one treatment plan that will work for all individuals. The healing process takes patience and determination.

If we were to get well, we might have to deal with the problems that depressed us in the first place. The complications we can avoid because we are ill would have to be recognized and dealt with. The very thought seems daunting.

When people ask me how I got well, I don't say, "I ignited my desire." What I do say is, "Sheer grit." As you know, that's not quite true. Rather "sheer grit" is a description of the effort I put into talk therapy and honest prayer to get better, especially initially because depression wants to keep you in its grip.

After my primary care doctor suggested I see a psychiatrist and made the appointment for me, I went home and pulled weeds. As beads of perspiration popped out on my forehead and sweat ran down my face, it seemed like I was pulling something outside of me just as I was pulling weeds out of the hard ground. Some dark, hideous plant called depression had taken root, fanned out, and grown inside me. Now it was time to get rid of it.

As I pulled out parts of this hideous plant, I could feel inner space being cleared. I couldn't jerk the whole plant out, but I could feel enough freedom to know I wanted more. I didn't want to go back to thinking and feeling the way I had. Some shift took place in me that very day. I knew I needed to work hard to keep that hideous plant pruned back and eventually pulled out for good. To do that, I was going to have to make some changes. No one was going to swoop in and rescue me; if I got well, it was going to be up to me.

Bringing about changes in one's thinking is never easy. But that day in the heat, the hideous plant started shriveling, and I intuitively knew if I tried hard enough I could eventually get rid of it. As Jesus said to the sick man by the pool, "Get up, pick up your mat, and walk" (v. 8), that's what I had to do. I had to pick myself up and start walking toward freedom. The man Jesus questioned "immediately . . . got well" (v. 9). I didn't get well right away, but I was on my way because I *wanted* to get well.

DAY 14

FOUR STRENGTH BUILDERS

Elijah was the same kind of person as we are.

—JAMES 5:17

HAVE you ever thought of yourself as being like Elijah? For a long time, I didn't. I marveled at his courage to speak the truth to King Ahab, his daring duel with the Baal prophets on Mount Carmel, and the physical stamina he had for running. Under the power of the Lord, he beat a chariot, running ahead of it for 15 miles! I could see no connection between us until I recognized we both struggled with our thoughts and emotions. My depression developed over time while Elijah's appeared to surface at a time of great fear. He was running away from Queen Jezebel. She wanted him killed because Elijah had killed her prophets (see 1 Kings 19:1–2).

To escape from Jezebel, "Elijah walked a whole day into the wilderness. He stopped and sat down in the shade of a tree" (v. 4). While he rested, Elijah pieced together all the events that led to this moment, including the threat on his life and his keen disappointment that challenging the prophets of Baal seemed to have accomplished nothing. The black bile of depression surfaced, and it was awful to experience. "'It's too much, LORD,' he prayed. 'Take away my life; I might as well be dead!'" (v. 4).

God tenderly responded to Elijah's prayer. It wasn't a response that immediately changed Elijah or his situation; it wasn't as if everything were suddenly OK, but it was a beginning. What Elijah did, and what God did, reveal several things that can help us deal with our depression.

Rest. After Elijah prayed, "he lay down under the tree and fell asleep" (v. 5). Elijah expended great physical energy in contest with the prophets of Baal, in the killing of them, in climbing Mount Carmel, and then in racing King Ahab back to Jerusalem. Elijah was on foot and King Ahab was in a chariot (see 1 Kings 18)! Then in trying to escape from Jezebel's threat on his life, he walked a whole day (1 Kings 19:4). For some of us, the frenzy of our lives or the numerous responsibilities we have may contribute to our depression. Our bodies may get weary just as Elijah's did. Physically he needed to recover; his body was saying, "I need rest." Our depression may be our body's way of saying the same thing.

Eat. While Elijah was sleeping, "an angel touched him and said, 'Wake up and eat'" (v. 5). Elijah "looked around and saw a loaf of bread and a jar of water near his head. He ate and drank, and lay down again. The LORD's angel returned and woke him up a second time, saying, 'Get up and eat, or the trip will be too much for you'" (vv. 6–7). The trip ahead was to a holy mountain where Elijah would converse with God. He would need strength to make the trip.

Some of us may need nourishing food to complete the road to recovery. "The food gave him enough strength to walk forty days to Sinai, the holy mountain" (v. 8).

Food is the fuel that keeps our brains and bodies working properly. We may have skipped meals or relied on junk food to deal with ongoing stress. Or now that we are depressed, we may not be motivated to eat well, so we rely on quick pick-me-ups. We may skip meats and vegetables in favor of sweets and caffeinated drinks. We may need to change our diet and even ask someone to help us if we want physical strength and mental clarity to deal with our depression.

Exercise. Elijah's recovery involved walking: walking with his servant to Beersheba, walking a whole day after that without his servant, and walking 40 days to Sinai, the holy mountain. Walking or physical exercise of any kind fights the passivity that often goes with depression. It increases energy, cuts tension, and increases optimism for many people.

Exercise also releases feel-good brain chemicals that may ease depression, reduces immune system chemicals that can worsen depression, and increases body temperature, which may have a calming effect. Perhaps Elijah needed this calming effect; after all, he was agitated! He was already in good physical shape because he was a runner, but walking was not competition. It allowed him to slow his thoughts as he paced himself. It allowed him to quiet himself for the spiritual work ahead.

Talk. After Elijah arrived at Mount Sinai, God asked him, "Elijah, what are you doing here?" (v. 9). God was giving Elijah an opportunity to vent his feelings, and that's what Elijah did: "Lord God Almighty, I have always served you— you alone. But the people of Israel have broken their covenant with you . . . and killed all your prophets. I am the only one left—and they are trying to kill me!" (v. 10). God asked Elijah the same question a second time, encouraging Elijah to continue talking, and he did until he was free of his feelings and ready to return to his role as prophet (see vv. 13–15).

Like Elijah, those crushing emotions or the spiritual perplexities we experience need to be released. Andrew Solomon in his atlas on depression, *The Noonday Demon,* says, "When I am asked, as I am constantly, about how best to treat depression, I tell people to talk about it . . . to keep articulating their feelings." Talking externalizes our problems where we can get a better look at them. Talking brings emotional relief, and having someone listen to us raises our hope level.

Resting, eating, exercising, and talking are four actions that facilitated Elijah's recovery. More was involved before he could be ready to serve God again as a prophet, but these four actions are highlighted because they are simple and because they are strength builders. We can understand these actions. When we take these actions—all of them or one or two of them—we will find our strength increasing. Like Elijah, we'll be ready for what's ahead on the road to recovery.

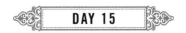

WHEN IMPOSSIBLE
BECOMES POSSIBLE

The LORD says, "Forget what happened before, and do not
think about the past. Look at the new thing I am going to do."

—ISAIAH 43:18–19 NCV

WITH depression, our emotions, thoughts, and heartaches may become so tightly intertwined that we see no way out. Our situation truly looks impossible, but is it?

To keep my sense of possibility functioning, I like to recall from time to time an account of women in a refugee camp along the Thai border in the 1980s. A cloud of impossibility hung over them. In fact, if I didn't know the ending of the story, and was just looking at the circumstances of their depression, I would say, "Those women will never recover," and they may not have if it hadn't been for Nuon Phaly.

Nuon Phaly was working for the Cambodian government when the Communist Khmer Rouge seized the capitol city Phnom Penh in 1975. Nuon, her husband, daughter, son, and two sisters were ousted from their home along with multitudes of Cambodians—3 million people— and marched to the countryside.

At the time, Nuon was pregnant with her third child. After marching for five days, Nuon gave birth on the side of a road. Her captors made her get up and keep walking. Over time, Nuon's husband, newborn baby, and two sisters all died. Laboring in the jungles of northeastern Cambodia, Nuon and her children never slept in the same place twice. They picked leaves and dug roots to feed themselves. Her daughter was sent to work in a youth camp and was forced at age 14 to marry a Khmer Rouge soldier.

When Khmer Rouge lost control of Cambodia, Nuon and her daughter and son returned to the province of Pursat near the capital city. They had been in the jungle for almost three and a half years. Her daughter soon gave birth to her first child, the product of her forced marriage. Nuon was able to locate some of her family, including her parents and youngest brother. Only two of Nuon's six siblings survived. Nuon also reconnected with a former classmate, and they got married.

Life, though, in Phnom Penh was chaotic and unsettled. Consequently, in 1984, Nuon and her family fled to a refugee camp on the Thai border. They hoped this would be a route to a new life. It was, but not in the way they expected.

Nuon and her husband joined a research project to document the experiences of their fellow camp members. This alerted them to the many orphans in the camp and to the many women who were traumatized by war, torture, and family separation. The women were unable to cope. They didn't move, they didn't talk, and they didn't take care of their children.

Nuon worried the women would die from depression if something wasn't done, so putting aside her own needs, she did something. Actually, she did several things.

She listened to their stories. Every depressed woman in the camp had a story to tell, a story of horrible experiences they endured in the war. One by one, Nuon sat with a woman, often for up to three hours at a time, and listened to her story. She made regular follow-up visits, listening more, until she gained the trust of the depressed woman.

She taught the women to forget. In *The Noonday Demon*, Andrew Solomon quotes Nuon as saying, "We have exercises we do each day, so that each day they can forget a little more of the things they will never forget entirely. During this time, I try to distract them with music or with embroidery or weaving, with concerts, with an occasional hour of television, with whatever seems to work, whatever they tell me they like. Depression is under the skin, all the surface of the body has the depression just below it, and we cannot take it out; but we can try to forget the depression even though it is right there." Her approach was similar to Isaiah's. He said to

God's people in exile, "Forget what happened before, and do not think about the past" (Isaiah 43:18 NCV).

She taught them to work. It is not enough just to forget, as helpful as that it is. The women needed to "look at the new thing" (v. 19 NCV), to have a future, so Nuon taught the women to work. She found ways to train them: some to clean houses, some to take care of children, and others to sew. Nuon knew the women must learn to do things, to do them well, and to have pride in what they did if they were going to make a life for themselves.

She taught them to love. She did this by having the women give manicures and pedicures to each other. While they filed each other's nails and applied nail polish, they began to talk to each other. In this way, they learned they could trust one another. As a by-product, they learned how to make friends so that they would never have to be so lonely again. They began to tell each other their stories, which they had told to no one but Nuon. This connection broke the emotional and physical isolation that goes along with depression.

In time many of the women resumed productive lives outside the camp. Nuon, though, noticed the number of children in the camp needing help continued to increase. When Nuon and her husband returned to Cambodia in 1993, they were accompanied by nine widows (women she had trained to take care of children!) and 91 orphaned children. This was the beginning of the Future Light Orphanage. It provided—and still does—care for orphans and families.

I trust her story will increase your hope and encourage you to dream about the new things God can do in your life. Through Nuon Phaly's caring concern and guidance, what appeared as impossible cases of depression were resolved. Recovery was possible.

DAY 16

CLEANING OUT
THE CLAY POT

My heart breaks when I remember the past.

—Psalm 42:4

A s A plant person, one thing I've had a hard time understanding is why I need to wash out a used clay pot in between plantings. Why do I need a clean pot if I'm going to put *dirt* in it?

I've learned a clean pot provides a healthy environment for a plant to grow. Because clay pots are porous, they absorb water. This is a good thing, but they also absorb minerals from the soil and chemicals from fertilizers. The porous material also provides a welcoming place for mold and fungus to grow.

It's essential, then, for the pot to be cleaned. The mineral deposits, chemical residue, fungus, and mold must go for a plant to have a healthy space in which to grow. Whether you're planting something new or rescuing an unhealthy plant, the pot needs to be cleaned for a fresh start.

Either way, the pot needs some work because of its past.

We've been comparing hope to a plant, mostly as a little sprout in need of attention. For some time now, we've noticed the plant isn't thriving; our depression indicates that. The plant droops; the leaves are turning yellow and dropping off, and it isn't growing. What might be causing this? It may have to do with the past—what's been deposited there. As the psalmist, the one who asked, "Why am I so depressed?" said, "My heart breaks when I remember the past" (Psalm 42:4).

Deeply dispirited, the psalmist contrasted past joys (when he led the pilgrim throng to the Temple) with the unhappy present (when enemies taunted him). He longed for the return of his former happy conditions. He wished he were back in Jerusalem where he could worship on the holy mountain.

It's not unusual to keep replaying what we perceive causes our depression. Like the psalmist, we relive yesterday's hurts and mistakes. The longer we do this, the more attached they are to our inner space, making them harder to remove.

Cleaning our inner space in order for hope to thrive is much more difficult than cleaning out a clay pot. Not much is needed for cleaning a clay pot: some water and a brush, some soap maybe, and even some bleach if mold is present. The process is simple, but cleaning our inner space is much more complicated.

Jake was haunted by a tragic incident in his past. His best friend was brutally and senselessly murdered. Memories of their times together kept filling Jake's head long past a typical grieving time. He grieved the loss of this friendship. And he was angry that someone would murder such a good person for no reason. While Jake didn't witness the killing, what he was told about it created vivid pictures in his mind—pictures he replayed over and over. At times, he even wished the worst for the killer—that someone would kill him! Consequently, Jake became a prisoner to rage and depression. The past haunted him so much he had to quit his job. As depression ate away at him, it also affected his family and marriage.

When his wife threatened to leave him, he finally decided something needed to be done. The grime, mold, and mineral deposits must be removed! Even though he was now motivated, "cleaning the pot" was a long process. He learned about different kinds of therapies and participated in group therapy for eight months. He consulted with a doctor and took antidepressants. He confessed his rage and anger to his pastor. He joined a Bible study group and disciplined himself to pray daily. Eventually he came to terms with the past. He accepted what he could not change and returned to work. Hope for him was now a viable plant. It wasn't a large plant, but it was a growing plant. And Jake had confidence that it would survive and thrive.

As awful as it was, Jake could at least link his depression to a specific event; however, sometimes causes from our past may be harder to identify. Old hurts from years past, such as how you were bullied in high school, guilt over mistakes you made, and feeling like you were an unwanted child, can dampen the present. Like mineral deposits, things like these attach themselves to the walls of our inner space, where they have every intention of staying permanently, and they will unless we raise our consciousnesses and do some hard cleaning.

The psalmist's cry about his heart breaking when he remembered the past is a cue for us to ask if our past has something to do with our depression. We may need the help of a therapist or counselor to answer this question. Whatever means we use to answer this question, if we answer yes, a thorough cleaning is in order. It may be painful; it may take time, tears, and numerous tools, but cleaning will be worth the effort. Hope will be revived by creating an environment that encourages a plant to thrive.

DAY 17

TAKING ACTION

Pick up your mat and walk.

—John 5:8 NIV

A MONG the symptoms of depression are:
- loss of interest in things you used to enjoy
- fatigue, tiredness, feeling run-down, loss of energy
- feeling like it is too much trouble to move around
- discouraged and pessimistic thoughts
- inability to concentrate, focus, remember, or make decisions

With symptoms like these, you can understand why a person might slide into what psychiatrist and author Dr. David D. Burns calls in his book *Feeling Good: The New Mood Therapy*, "do-nothingism." This condition may start as simple procrastination. You stop making your bed, you don't wash your hair, and the laundry piles up. Left unchecked, this procrastination can morph into a person feeling completely overwhelmed by the urge to do nothing. But it can be curbed by doing something. Action is often important to recovery, as the Bible illustrates.

Jesus' commands. Jesus did not have a canned approach to healing. He didn't go through the same motions or say the same words every time. Commands were often part of the healing process.

To the man who was sick for 38 years, Jesus said, "Get up! Pick up your mat and walk" (John 5:8 NIV).

To the paralyzed man whose friends brought him to Jesus for healing, He said, "I tell you, get up, pick up your mat, and go home!" (Mark 2:11).

To the deaf man who wanted ears to hear, Jesus said, "'*Ephphatha*,' which means, 'Open up!'" (Mark 7:34).

To the man who had been born blind, He said, "Go and wash your face in the Pool of Siloam" (John 9:7).

To the man who had died—and had been dead for four days—Jesus said, "Lazarus, come forth" (John 11:43 KJV).

On these occasions, Jesus' instructions to act seemed to be part of the healing process, as if movement were needed for the recipient to fully claim his healing.

Naomi's idea. When the widows, Naomi and Ruth, arrived in Bethlehem, Naomi was a bitter, depressed woman. Ruth looked after them by going to the fields and gleaning grain left by the harvesters. Naomi seems to have shut down, as if there were nothing she could have done. When Ruth returned with an abundance of grain, Naomi's mood changed as she realized something could be done. She asked Ruth, "Where did you gather all this grain today? Whose field have you been working in? May God bless the man who took an interest in you!" (Ruth 2:19). When Ruth told her the man was Boaz, one of Naomi's relatives, Naomi started making plans for arranging a marriage between Boaz and Ruth. Their problems would be solved! The woman who once blamed God for causing her affliction changed her attitude. She exclaimed to Ruth, "The LORD always keeps his promises to the living and the dead" (v. 20).

Elijah's work. When Elijah was holed up in a cave, feeling sorry for himself, God said to him, "*Go* out and *stand* before me on top of the mountain" (1 Kings 19:11, author's emphasis). There God revealed Himself to Elijah in a way He hadn't before. God was getting Elijah spiritually ready to rejoin life and resume his role as prophet. God told Elijah to return to his ministry as a prophet and appoint others to be prophets too.

Elijah's healing would not have been complete if the process had stopped somewhere earlier. This is a man with a sense of God's calling; this is a man who needed to act to be fully whole.

These biblical incidents remind us of the value action has in healing and recovery. This is certainly true for those who have "do-nothingism." The natural antidote is to do *something*. As simple as this sounds, it is challenging for those who are depressed. Since we don't feel like doing anything, we assume we can't. This is our reality. We feel it; therefore, it must be true. It is true in the sense that we're not ready to run a marathon, clean out the garage, or even clean off a cluttered desk. Taking some kind of action, though, will break the power of "do-nothingism." The action we take doesn't have to be huge, impressive, or complete to diminish its power over us.

If we think we can't exercise, we can try walking 50 feet.

If we think we couldn't possibly clean out the garage, we can start by cleaning one corner. If that is too much, we can clean off one shelf.

If we feel overwhelmed by all the papers, magazines, pens, and bills spread out all over our desk, we could start with removing the magazines.

Taking action is beneficial because it disproves what we have been telling ourselves. Instead of thinking we can't do anything, we have verifiable evidence that we can do something. We can also take some pride in what we've done. At the end of the day, a time when we tend to think nothing was accomplished, we can remind ourselves, "Today I walked 50 feet," or "I managed to clean off a garage shelf." Noting our accomplishment reduces our sense of helplessness, affirming we can do something. This will encouraged us to do even more: walk 100 feet, clean three more shelves, or categorize the desk papers for filing.

Dr. Burns additionally found in *Feeling Good: The New Mood Therapy* "that the great majority of depressed patients referred to [him improved] substantially if they [tried] to help themselves." He said it hardly seemed to matter what a depressed person did, as long as he or she did something. Taking action will make a difference in the way we feel.

DAY 18

SHARING THE LOAD

*I will take some of the spirit
I have given you and give it to them.*

—Numbers 11:17

D OES your depression feel heavy? What kind of load are you carrying? Is it a work load? An emotional one? A spiritual one? Would you like some relief? Have you considered sharing the load? That's what God encouraged Moses to do when he was overwhelmed with the responsibility of leading the Israelites to the Promised Land.

When Moses admitted to God that his load was too much for him, God heard—and answered—Moses's honest prayer. God said to him,

> *Assemble seventy respected men who are recognized as leaders of the people, bring them to me at the Tent of my presence . . . and I will take some of the spirit I have given you and give it to them. Then they can help you bear the responsibility for these people, and you will not have to bear it alone.*
>
> *—Numbers 11:16–17*

God alerted Moses to the presence of other responsible people—people who could help him. There were 70 respected, recognizable leaders in the large group headed to the Promised Land. These men could help Moses.

God instructed Moses to take action. The leaders who could lighten Moses's load needed to be engaged. It was up to Moses to call them together. When he did, God planned to take some of the spirit He gave Moses and give it to them. Moses had the spirit of service, as well as a vision of what God was doing to redeem His people. He had been called to carry out a significant task. If others shared this spirit, they would catch the vision. They would help Moses bear the responsibility for all the people. Moses would still be *the* leader, but his load would be lighter.

Would you like a lighter load? Would you like to reduce the heaviness you're feeling? Have you considered following the wisdom inherent in God's words to Moses? Have you considered sharing your load?

Odd as it may sound, one way to do this is through talking. Perhaps you've noticed how we often use the word *sharing* when we mean *talking*. We use *share* when we have more than just an exchange of words in mind. We talk about the weather, but we share our feelings. In return, we want others to understand our situation. We want them to "get" what we are experiencing, and when they do, the heaviness will be reduced. A shared load is a lighter load.

The load is lighter because the inner pressure of troubling emotions has been released. Emotions such as anger, grief, and jealousy are powerful, and when we talk about these to others, the emotions lose some of their power. They no longer weigh as much. In addition, we gain the support of the people we share with and then we are stronger to cope with what's causing our depression.

Sharing that leads to a lighter load doesn't mean talking about the load all the time. It's not tossing out your problem and hoping it will land some place where help is available. Neither is a lighter load gained by talking to just anybody. It's talking to someone who will really listen.

Who might that person be? It could be a friend or a family member. It could be a fellow church member, a Bible study leader, or a counselor. It's not so much who a person is as it is his or her ability to hear, understand, and not be judgmental. It needs to be someone who knows life can sometimes be more than we can handle. It needs to be someone who won't give cliché responses to our pain.

Listeners like this may be just as hidden to you as the 70 respected leaders were to Moses, but they are there. Moses just needed to look around, identify them, and bring them together where God could talk to them. We need to do the same if we want to lighten our load.

Those more apt to listen sympathetically are people who have experienced disappointments in life and learned from their experiences. Once we identify them, we can approach them and say something like, "I'm not at my best right now. May I talk with you sometime? I need a sounding board, and I could use your prayers." To be considerate, you might request only an hour of the listener's time.

Most people will respond positively to a request like this, particularly if a length of time is specified. But if you don't want to approach someone—if the idea is just too daunting—then make an appointment to see a counselor or therapist.

I'll always be glad I saw a psychiatrist. After I told him what my husband and I had been through, he said, "You have reason to be depressed." Ah, here was my day in court! The evidence was examined by a judge, and his verdict was "not guilty." So many people had inferred that if I had enough faith, if I were strong enough as a Christian, then I would have had no reason to be depressed. Now here was someone competent and knowledgeable, who could appreciate our ideals and our efforts in life, and see why I had become depressed. What a relief! I was still depressed, but its heaviness was reduced. My load was lighter and my hope brighter as I drove home that day because it was a shared load.

DAY 19

VITAL CONNECTIONS

We have placed our hope in [God] . . . as you help us.

—2 CORINTHIANS 1:10–11

E LIJAH, who had been so involved with many people, including the 400 Baal prophets, curious onlookers, King Ahab, and Queen Jezebel, needed solitude to recover from the symptoms he battled. Martin Luther, though, who battled depression himself, said people who are depressed need to be with others.

He wrote, "Seek out some Christian brother, some wise counselor. Undergird yourself with the fellowship of the church." Dining together, singing, and talking with friends interrupts a person's ruminating. Being with others takes away feelings of alienation and loneliness that sometimes accompany depression. Having people in our lives can help us deal with depression, as these three biblical examples illustrate.

Practical, survival help. What would Naomi have done without Ruth's help? When Naomi decided to return to her former home in Bethlehem after the deaths of her husband and sons, she would have had to travel alone, not a wise thing for a woman to do in that day and time. But on that long journey back, Naomi had Ruth's companionship. They could ruminate on the past and consider possibilities for the future. Ruth stood by Naomi even as she exclaimed in Bethlehem how God had made her life bitter. Ruth patiently committed herself to helping Naomi, who seemed paralyzed by her emotions. She did nothing. It was Ruth who went to the fields to glean grain. It was the successfulness of this gleaning that gave Naomi a burst of insight on how their destitute state could change. When there was no one else, Ruth was there for Naomi.

Emotional support. Dorcas was a good woman who "spent all her time doing good and helping the poor" (Acts 9:36). In particular, she sewed clothes for them.

Dorcas lived in Joppa, a city on the Mediterranean Sea coast. The sea was a perilous place at that time. Many men went to sea and never returned. They left behind bereaved and usually destitute widows. Dorcas reached out to them, befriended them, and possibly even asked them to join her in doing good works. I believe this because twice in Dorcas's story, the widows are referred to specifically.

After Dorcas died, the believers sent for Peter who was in a nearby town. When he arrived in Joppa, the Bible specifically notes, "all *the widows* crowded around him, crying and showing him all the shirts and coats that Dorcas had made" (v. 39, author's emphasis).

After Peter prayed for Dorcas and told her to get up, "he called for the believers, especially the widows, and presented her to them alive" (v. 41 NIV). To refer to the widows as a separate group did not mean that the widows were not believers. It means that a distinct group had been formed, a group known as *the widows*.

Dorcas brought them together where they could bond and share their stories. She helped them deal with their grief by providing them an opportunity to interact with others and giving them something to do. When they needed a lifeline, Dorcas threw one. She knew being with other women would raise their hope and increase their inner strength. No wonder they were so upset when she died. She had been their lifeline.

Prayers and presence. Paul counted on the prayers and presence of others to help keep his hope healthy. When he wrote his second letter to the Corinthians, he had just been in Asia where he had experienced hardships. No one knows exactly what those hardships were, but he did say he was "under great pressure, far beyond [his] ability to endure" (1:8 NIV). The pressure was so great that he "despaired of life itself" (v. 8 NIV) and "felt . . . the sentence of death" (v. 9 NIV).

While the distress weighed Paul down, he didn't stay down. He wrote, "From such terrible dangers of death [God] saved us, and will save us; and we have placed our hope in him that he will save us again, as you help us *by means of your prayers for us*" (vv. 10–11, author's emphasis). Their prayers helped Paul set his hope on God.

While he was in Asia, Paul wrote a stern letter via Titus to the Corinthian believers. He had no idea how they would receive his reprimand, so he anxiously awaited Titus's return. While he waited, his "flesh had no rest" and he had "conflicts without, fears within" (2 Corinthians 7:5 NASB). When Titus finally returned, he told Paul the Corinthians had no hard feelings toward him. Paul was relieved and wrote the Corinthians saying, "God, who comforts the depressed, comforted us by the coming of Titus" (v. 6 NASB). Titus's presence and his report comforted and reassured Paul.

I can't tell you which is best for you—solitude or people—but I know from experience both help me.

When I'm around people, I'm alert to their needs and to what response I should make. Solitude provides a refreshing break when I don't have to be alert. I can rest and recover. Solitude also gives me uninterrupted time to think. This is when I can analyze why I feel the way I feel. Most importantly, solitude helps me connect with God. I can share with Him my concerns and seek His guidance for day-by-day living and be reassured that He has a purpose for my life.

But I also know I need people. Other people support, comfort, and encourage us. They reduce the loneliness that comes with depression and help us see solutions we aren't aware of. They pray for us, check on us, and sometimes reassure us we are worthwhile human beings. Most importantly, they increase our hope level. Hope grows when we network together, so I would have to agree with Luther—fellowship meals are important!

DAY 20

WHEN HOPE
NEEDS A HAND

All we like sheep have gone astray.

—Isaiah 53:6 KJV

SHEEP are not strong, independent animals. They are easily frightened and prone to wander. That's why sheep need shepherds to guide, protect, and even rescue them at times. One particular time sheep need rescuing is when they become cast down. According to Phillip Keller, a shepherd and writer, *cast down* is an old English shepherd's term for a sheep that has turned over on its back and cannot get up again by itself.

Keller explains how a sheep might find itself in this position. When wandering away from the fold, a sheep might lie down in some little hollow in the ground to rest. If he rolls over on his side to stretch, his body's center of gravity shifts. If he turns too far so that its feet can no longer touch the ground, then it is almost impossible for him to get up again. The sheep panics and paws frantically. This only makes things worse, and it rolls over even farther. He needs a shepherd to pick him up and set his feet on solid ground.

Some of us who are depressed become cast down. In fact, that's the word the King James Version uses to describe the experience of the psalmist who asked, "Why am I so depressed? (Psalms 42:5, 11; 43:5 HCSV). In the King James Version, that question reads, "Why art thou cast down, O my soul?"

Cast down is an apt term for what some of us experience. Our depression goes on for so long or worsens in such away that our center is thrown off. We're in a hole and can't get out on our own. We need a shepherd (a professional of some kind) who, metaphorically speaking, has his or her hand stretched out, offering help. We need to grab hold of that hand so we can get out of our cast down place.

That person might be a counselor, a psychologist, a therapist, a nurse practitioner, a social worker, a primary care physician, or a psychiatrist. These people are trained to help.

The problem, though, may be our unwillingness to reach for the hand and let him or her help us out of the hole. People who are seriously depressed often resist treatment.

We might resist because of that "do-nothingism" we mentioned on Day 17. We just don't feel like making a call, taking the time to see a mental health professional, or checking in with our doctor.

We might hesitate because of the pessimism that often accompanies depression. We say, "It won't really do any good."

It could be fear. We are afraid we may have to do something out of our comfort range.

Or maybe we don't want anyone to know we are depressed. Some attach a stigma to mental illness that isn't associated with other types of medical conditions.

The world of talk therapy, or any kind of therapy, may seem like a strange land. We don't know what will happen there. What kinds of questions will be asked? What kind of "odd" thing might occur?

We may be reluctant to talk about our feelings. We keep things to ourselves, and we don't want to open up to a stranger. That would be like losing our protective shield and exposing ourselves.

As valid as we may think those reasons seem, the fact remains that we are in a deep hole. If we've been there for a while and can't get out on our own, we may need to do what the great Syrian general Naaman did: try something we'd rather not do.

When Naaman noticed strange white spots on his body, he knew he had the awful disease of leprosy. No one in Syria knew anyone who could cure leprosy, not even the king, who was also troubled by Naaman's discovery. The king valued this great general.

The little girl who lived in Naaman's home, though, knew someone who could cure leprosy. She wasn't a Syrian;

she was an Israelite. The Syrians had taken her captive in a raid, and she was now a servant of Naaman's wife. The girl hadn't forgotten her Israeli heritage. "She said to her mistress, 'I wish that my master could go to the prophet who lives in Samaria! He would cure him of his disease'" (2 Kings 5:3).

When the king heard, he urged Naaman to see this prophet and provided the support he needed.

Elisha, God's prophet, was aware of Naaman's arrival in Samaria. He didn't, though, go out to see Naaman. He sent out his servant with a message telling Naaman to wash himself seven times in the Jordan River to be cured.

Naaman was furious. I can imagine him saying to himself, "This is no way to treat me. I'm an important general. I thought Elisha would come out, call on his God, wave his hand over my sores, and I would be healed. But no! He told me to bathe seven times in the Jordan River! Not me! I might as well have stayed home and bathed in the rivers there! At least our rivers are cleaner than the muddy Jordan." The whole idea repulsed him, so he turned around and went home.

His servants took all this in, and after a while they said to Naaman, "Sir, if the prophet had told you to do something difficult, you would have done it. Now why can't your just wash yourself, as he said, and be cured?" (v. 13).

Finally, wallowing in the misery of his hopeless state, Naaman apparently thought to himself, *Well, why not?* He swallowed his pride and went back to the muddy Jordan. He took off his clothes and waded into the water. He ducked under once, twice . . . seven times. When he came out of the river, the leprosy was gone! The very thing he didn't want to do was the very thing he needed to do to be healed.

Sometimes it pays to do what's uncomfortable or frightening to bring about change in our situation. Taking hold of a professional's hand may be the very thing we need to do to get out of our cast down place.

DAY 21

THE POWER
OF EXPECTATION

To have faith is to be sure of the things we hope for.

—Hebrews 11:1

I N A newspaper article I once read, a woman with depression told how she tried for months to get better. When she didn't get better, she went to her doctor who prescribed an antidepressant. She said, "After taking one pill, I immediately felt better."

I question the woman's experience. At the time she made this statement, antidepressants did not bring quick relief. They took days or even weeks to start showing results. What I suspect happened is the woman expected the antidepressant to help her, so it did. She experienced what is called the placebo effect.

A placebo is anything that seems to be authentic medical treatment, but isn't. Most often, researchers use placebos during clinical drug studies to help understand the effects a new drug might have on a particular condition. For example, some people in a study might be given a new drug to reduce anxiety. Others would get a placebo such as a sugar pill or a vitamin. None of the people in the study would know whether they were getting the real drug or the placebo.

A percentage of people recover by taking placebos—medication presented to them as the real thing. One of the most common theories as to why a placebo works is that it is due to a person's expectations. If a person anticipates a pill will do something, then it's possible their body's chemistry could induce effects similar to what authentic medication might have caused. This response is not something that's imaginary or fake. Actual changes occur in the brain and body.

This doesn't mean that everyone responds this way to a placebo. If they did, we wouldn't have to worry about discovering more antidepressants! Placebos have their limitations; however, there is enough evidence of their success to help us appreciate the power of expectations.

What our doctor says and how he says it also influences expectations. Your medicine will probably work better if your doctor listens to your physical complaints and gives you a pep talk about the medicine he is prescribing.

Similarly, patients have more side effects from a new medication when their doctor warns them they may occur. If people expect to experience headaches, nausea, or drowsiness, there is a greater chance of those reactions happening.

Even having choices about medications makes a difference. People respond better if they are allowed to choose among different medications that do the same thing. This increases the effectiveness of the selected drug and reduces possible side effects.

Placebos, pep talks, and choices show the power of expectations. They impact our brains and our bodies. This shouldn't be a surprise to believers. We are people of faith. We know about the power of expectancy. With faith in God, we believe things can happen and anticipate their happening.

This doesn't mean all believers have an equal amount of faith. Some of us have the gift of faith that Paul mentions in 1 Corinthians 12:9. I did not receive this gift! We are all at various stages on the faith spectrum, some having lots of faith, others not so much, and still others somewhere in between. But if we are believers, we have *some* faith. And if we work with what we have, we can raise our hope level.

Sheer grit, as I mentioned earlier, played an important role in my recovery, especially in the months after my diagnosis. I believed I could make changes within.

I believed talking was therapeutic, so I was willing to see a psychiatrist. I expected him to help me, and he did.

I believed honest praying could make a difference, so I prayed, "Father, how could you do this to me and my family? How could you treat us this way?"

I believed a particular type of praying could reclaim my belief that God had a purpose for my life, something you'll hear more about in Day 24.

While you couldn't say I had a strong faith, I had some faith—faith that empowered a sense of expectancy about the tools I chose to use. Those tools assisted in my recovery.

Fortunately, many tools are available. The success of whatever tool or tools we use to fight depression *may* depend on the power of our expectations, so what do you expect? Do you believe seeing a psychiatrist will help? What about antidepressants? Will prayer? Will exercise? Will biofeedback? Will diet? It's not my expectations that will make a difference in your recovery, it's yours.

As the writer of Hebrews reminds us, faith and hope are related: "Faith is confidence in what we hope for and assurance about what we do not see" (11:1 NIV). One provides support, and the other gives us momentum. Faith is our foundation, our now; hope is our expectation, our future.

HOW DARK CAN
THE DARK BE?

He said to Jesus, "Remember me,
Jesus, when you come as King!"

—LUKE 23:42

WILLIAM Cowper was an English poet who lived during the eighteenth century. You might know him best as the author of some great hymns. Here are some lines from some of his hymns:

"God moves in a mysterious way,
His wonders to perform."

"There is a fountain filled with blood,
Drawn from Immanuel's veins;
And sinners, plunged beneath that flood,
Lose all their guilty stain."

"Oh, for a closer walk with God,
A calm and heavenly frame,
A light to shine upon the road,
That leads me to the Lamb!"

"Let everlasting thanks be Thine,
For such a bright display,
That makes a world of darkness shine,
With beams of heavenly day."

If all you had to go on were these words, what would you conclude about Cowper? That he had a solid relationship with God? That he had a close walk with Him? That his life was filled with brightness as he walked in the light? In actuality, he often walked in darkness. In fact, his story shows just how dark depression can become.

Cowper experienced times of awful torment, despair, hallucinations, and even attempted suicide. When he was unsuccessful in killing himself, he sensed God's wrath. He was certain he had committed an unpardonable sin. Within a few weeks, he suffered a complete break from reality.

Cowper's brother took him to an asylum run by an evangelical clergyman who had studied medicine. For the next six months, Cowper suffered terrible visions and heard voices but finally grew calmer under the minister's care.

While Cowper was at the asylum, his brother assured him he could be forgiven, that he could be saved. Cowper was converted and made an almost instantaneous recovery. We wish his story could end there, but that is not the case. His days got even darker.

After about a year, Cowper moved in with a family who shared his religious convictions. When the husband was killed in a fall from a horse, Cowper remained in the household. Eventually, he and the widow made plans to marry.

As the date for the wedding drew closer, Cowper's mental condition worsened. He suffered another attack of severe depression. He went to live with his friend the reverend John Newton, author of "Amazing Grace." The two were collaborating on a collection of hymns. Cowper stayed with Newton for the next 13 months.

Cowper made more suicide attempts. He claimed God was commanding him to sacrifice his life. When his friends intervened, Cowper felt God condemning him to eternal punishment for trying to commit suicide. His psychotic delusions gradually faded, but his sense of being excluded from God's mercy never did. Everyone else could experience the mercy and grace of God; he was the lone exception.

Eventually Cowper went into a deep depression from which he never recovered. Though still cared for by friends, he died believing he had offended God and was beyond forgiveness.

Some people question whether Cowper's mental illness was depression. They want to call it something else, but advanced depression can have these symptoms. Knowing this should be an incentive for us to help ourselves, seek the help of others, and seek God's help. If we were diagnosed with heart disease or diabetes, we would change our lifestyle in order to live healthier. An episode of depression might mean we need to make some changes in how we think.

One thing we can do is question the "the certainties of despair." In his book, *When the Darkness Will Not Lift*, pastor John Piper says, "Despair is relentless in the certainties of its pessimism." In Cowper's case, the certainty was that he could not be forgiven. When a belief like this surfaces in our mind, we should address it before it grows, solidifies, and inflicts long-term damage. We need to allow for the possibility that we might be wrong about some things and be willing to make corrections.

Cowper's story speaks to me in a special way. It reminds me that I *am* forgiven. I can't tell you the number of times I've been reassured by standing with fellow Christians and singing "The dying thief rejoiced to see that fountain in his day; and there may I, though vile as he, wash all my sins away." As we sing, we are reassured of what Cowper could never grasp—that we aren't beyond receiving God's forgiveness.

What means the most to me is God still used Cowper in spite of his illness. His words live on and influence people's faith year after year. This tells me that no matter what trauma I've gone through or what mistakes I've made, God can still use me. Something meaningful, purposeful, or enduring can still come out of my life, and it can out of yours too.

Cowper's darkness never took away the possibility of his producing something that would bless thousands of Christians by giving them words to articulate their faith. God can do the same with our lives. Depression is not the end of us. Realizing this makes my "world of darkness shine with beams of heavenly" light. What does it do for your world?

DAY 23

THE HOLDING
POWER OF JESUS

You, Lord, keep my lamp burning.

—Psalm 18:28 NIV

I was born into a culture where children sang loudly and heartedly. We didn't always know the full meaning of the choruses we sang, but we sang with conviction. One of our favorites was "Give me oil in my lamp, keep me burning." At our church, we revised the line to "Give me oil in my lamp, keep me burning, burning, burning." We were earnest.

With what knowledge we had, we wanted to make sure we kept our lamps burning. The burning meant our service to God. Then, when I became a worker with children both in churches and in camps, we continued to sing this song with gusto. We meant what we sang.

In college, the "oil" in my life wasn't as plentiful, and the light in my lamp started flickering. In seminary, though, the light strengthened and burned brightly once I said to God, "Anyplace You want me to go, I'll go. Whatever You want me to do, I'll do it!" Before this decision, I felt like I *had* to serve God. Afterwards, I *wanted* to serve Him. And I never thought otherwise, until something happened that contributed to my depression.

My husband Bob was working as a registrar at a Christian university when he was fired the first time. We prayed and searched earnestly. After ten months, the only opening that came was with a nonaccredited Bible training center. Bob was hired as the registrar and as a teacher. He taught preaching, teaching, and speech—subjects Bob always had an interest in. He himself was an excellent communicator.

When the job at the Bible training center ended, he could not find another job in higher education. Bob wondered if God was channeling his love for preaching into a full-time ministry. We talked with our pastor about it, and he agreed with us. The pastor even said, "We're going to have some positions open up here, and one of those, I'm thinking, would be just right for you." We left the pastor's office feeling encouraged and confident.

One by one four positions in our church became available, and Bob was not hired for them, including one that would have been pastoring a mission near us. Early on in the planning for the mission, our church interviewed Bob for the position and included me in the conversation. All we were told afterwards was, "We're not ready to hire at this time." Hope lingered within us. We had a heart for missions, and we were already leading a Bible study in the area.

About 18 months later, the church made its selection for the mission pastorate. It was not Bob. When Bob didn't get the position, no one said a word to us—not the committee, not the pastor, not our friends, nor those in the adult Sunday School department we led.

I took their silence and rejection personally and concluded we had been stamped "unacceptable." Looking back, I can see this was where my depression began forming. I didn't realize it at the time because I didn't know that much about depression. All I knew was that a black mood developed.

I can also see now how I should have responded differently. I was putting too much emphasis on what others thought of me. I remember feeling so undone and fragile after being interviewed by the mission committee. While I had interviewed for jobs before—some I had gotten and some I hadn't—I had never been questioned about my faith or my service. I had never had to explain myself or defend my actions.

But if I had known and had a more mature response, I might have missed out on an experience that would end up forever keeping my lamp burning. As it was, I brooded about the way we were treated, and it was brooding that went on way too long. Every time I went to church or attended a Christian activity, I thought about all that happened, and darkness enveloped me. If I were away from church for a few days, my mood would brighten. It finally occurred to me that if I stopped going to church—if I gave up all my Christian activities—I could keep the darkness at bay.

I considered the Christian activities I could eliminate from my life. I would quit teaching Sunday School, and, of course, I would stop going to Sunday morning and Sunday evening worship services. I would drop the Bible study Bob and I were leading. And I wouldn't participate in midweek services or be involved in women's missions and ministries. I wouldn't help any longer with the organizing of the mission church. And that's when Jesus appeared.

The Holy Spirit gave me an image of Jesus. I saw Him dusty and bloody, carrying His Cross, wearing His crown of thorns, experiencing the ultimate rejection. With weary, sad eyes, He looked at me and said, "Brenda, I thought we were in this together." With those words and that look, I knew that I could never reject Him. I would never stop serving Him. I love Him far too much for that. Jesus kept my lamp burning when the winds of rejection threatened to snuff it out.

That picture of Jesus is the oil that keeps me burning, burning, burning to serve Him. Even during the darkest days of my depression, even when I felt as if my life had no purpose, I continued to serve. It's a picture I won't ever forget. Jesus keeps my lamp burning because He indelibly printed Himself on my soul.

DAY 24

MIND RENEWAL

Be ye transformed by the renewing of your mind.

—ROMANS 12:2 KJV

THE HOLDING power of Jesus, seeing a psychiatrist, asking myself questions, crying in the bathroom, and even trying new recipes all helped me get better, but there was one important thing I needed to work on if my recovery were to be complete. I needed God to renew my belief that He has a purpose for my life.

I wasn't absolutely certain how to proceed; I only knew something needed to be done. Fortunately, in a small church group, we had been studying a book called *Prayer Can Change Your Life* by Dr. William R. Parker and Elaine St. Johns. This old book offers a prayerful way to renew our minds through surrender and affirmation.

In surrender (or you might like to think of it as release), we give God all the rubbish that is within us—our fears, our guilt, our anger, our grief, our broken dreams, and our faulty assumptions. We cast all our cares on Him (see 1 Peter 5:7).

Already some releasing had been going on with those tearful, honest prayers in the bathroom, but now it was time for a more thorough inner cleaning. There was some residue still hanging on: unforgiveness, disappointment, grief over the past, self-pity, and worry over the future, among other things. I reached around inside and gathered all this up, similar to how you would clean the gunk out of a pumpkin so you could carve a smiling face.

I gave this gunk to God by praying something like this, "Lord, I give You my disappointments, my grief, and my despair. I forgive the people I believe hurt us. I give You the past. I release it to You."

Once the release of rubbish is accomplished, it is important not to quit praying, and here's why. The release, the cleaning out, creates an empty space that needs to be filled. If not, the unforgiveness, the grief, and possibly other negative emotions will return and take up residence. Jesus reminded us of this kind of thing in a story He told about an evil spirit leaving a person. The spirit travels over dry country, looking for a place to rest. If the evil spirit can't find a resting place, "it says to itself, 'I will go back to my house'" (Matthew 12:44). The evil spirit goes back and finds the house he left clean and tidy. Then he goes out and brings home seven other spirits to live with him. "When it is all over, that person [who swept his house clean] is in worse shape than at the beginning" (v. 45).

I didn't want to be worse off. I was aiming to renew my mind, so I followed the release of the rubbish with affirmative prayer. In affirmative praying, we put helpful, creative thoughts into the empty space. We affirm the kind of person we want to be or what we truly want to believe. In my case, I affirmed that God had a purpose for my life even though I couldn't see what that purpose was.

My words went something like this: "Today, Lord, I see myself as being free of depression and free of hurt. I see myself as feeling good about life again. I see You smiling in approval of me because I remained faithful without understanding what was happening. I affirm my trust in You. I believe You have a purpose behind all that has happened and that You have a purpose for my life. I'm hopeful about the future."

Attempting to transform our minds through prayer, using surrender and affirmation, is not a one-time prayer experience. The first morning I prayed this way, the effects of it lasted about one hour. Then I was back wallowing in self-pity and hurt. The next morning, I prayed again in the same way. This time, the effect lasted a little longer. Morning by morning, I prayed this way until I sensed a difference in my mind and spirit.

When Gillian Marchenko, author of *Still Life: A Memoir of Living Fully with Depression*, was getting better, one of her children said to her, "I know that you are feeling better lately."

"Oh, really? How's that?"

"Because you are doing more at home with us. And because you sing while you do the dishes."

That's how I could tell too. One day I started singing, and I realized I hadn't sung like that in months. I smiled to myself, stopped washing the dishes, and said aloud, "God does have a purpose for my life!" What that was specifically, I didn't know. A purpose wasn't any more evident than it had been. What had changed was my belief. My mind was renewed.

My struggle with depression showed me that having a purpose for living is essential to my being spiritually and mentally healthy. For me that purpose has to be an eternal one. Living for something in this life is not enough. I need a purpose that makes sense out of the nonsense, that makes the humdrum and tedious palatable, that gets me beyond the disappointments of life.

Acknowledging God's realness and serving Him gives me a purpose. Aligning myself with His will makes even the insignificant details of life significant. Does this mean His purpose is always clear? No, I operate in the trust that a purpose is being worked out. I seldom miss a day without saying a prayer borrowed from Jeremiah, who also suffered from depression, "Great and mighty God, whose name is the LORD Almighty, great are your purposes and mighty are your deeds" (Jeremiah 32:18–19 NIV). To which I add, "And I know You, God, are working out a purpose for my life." I believe this, and I believe He's working out a purpose for your life too.

DAY 25

RAINDROPS OF PRAISE

Let us, then, always offer praise to God.

—Hebrews 13:15

R EMEMBER those raindrops that blew into my covered patio, the raindrops I mentioned on Day 1? They weren't numerous or large. If we had been sitting on the patio watching the rain, we probably wouldn't have noticed them, but they were enough to moisten the soil surrounding the what-appeared-to-be-dead fern. The power of the raindrops prompted new growth. The plant wasn't dead after all.

In the same way, praising God can activate and maintain hope. But this doesn't mean that attributing worth to God, showing Him our appreciation, and expressing our gratitude, is easy to do.

Praising God while depressed goes contrary to what we are feeling. We're not in an appreciative mood. No emotion of gratitude is rising up within us, begging to be expressed.

Praising God while depressed may be hard to do if we are blaming Him for our present circumstances, like Moses and Naomi did (see Day 9). It's hard to tell someone you are thankful for them when you think they are responsible for your troubles.

Our situation can be so stark that our focus becomes, "How can I manage?" or even, "How can I survive?" rather than thinking about and acknowledging God's good qualities.

When depressed, we are usually preoccupied with ourselves and our needs. It's hard to instead focus on God.

To praise God under these circumstances makes it a "sacrifice of praise" (Hebrews 13:15 KJV). We sacrifice our judgment, our view, our focus, and our feelings and make ourselves do what does not come naturally.

We make this sacrifice with "the fruit of our lips giving thanks to his name" (v. 15 KJV). If we verbally express our thanks, this will increase our confidence that we really are speaking to Someone who is real.

Because we don't feel like praising God, we may be short on words or can't think of anything to say.

One option is to begin simply, "Thank You, Lord, that I have a voice and can give thanks to You." "Thank You, Lord, that I have shelter." "Thank You, Lord, that I am alive."

Or borrow someone else's words, such as those of some of the psalmists. Write them on a card, and repeat them out loud several times throughout each day.

> LORD, *you are my God; I will give you thanks forever.*
> —*Psalm 30:12*

> LORD, *I know you will never stop being merciful to me. Your love and loyalty will always keep me safe.*
> —*Psalm 40:11*

Even a simple phrase will work. During one of my lowest points, I borrowed a phrase from one of Jesus' prayers. I simply didn't have the words myself.

I wasn't emotionally or spiritually ready to encourage Bob after he lost his job at the Bible training center. With the first job loss, I expressed confidence in him, in God, and in the future. But with the second loss, I didn't see much of a future for us. Who was going to hire somebody who lost two jobs so close together?

I was studying Jesus' prayer life at the time for a book I was writing. I noticed gratitude was an integral part of Jesus' prayer life in good times and bad.

When the 70 men Jesus sent out to Judean villages and towns returned, they spoke of how successful their ministry trip had been. To their surprise, they found that people listened, healings occurred, and demons submitted to them in the name of Jesus.

Jesus shared in their joy. He prayed, "I thank thee, O Father, Lord of heaven and earth, that thou hast hid these things from the wise and prudent, and hast revealed them unto babes: even so, Father; for so it seemed good in thy sight" (Luke 10:21 KJV).

He said this same prayer after the people of Chorazin, Bethsaida, and Capernaum disregarded Him and refused to repent. Jesus reacted by pronouncing woes on these cities and prayed the very same prayer (see Matthew 11:25–26 KJV).

I marveled that Jesus did this, that He could be so thankful during a time of rejection. I couldn't bring myself to say, "Thank You, Father, that Bob lost his job. Thank You that we are in this dilemma." I wasn't thankful, and I didn't expect to ever be thankful.

I was drawn, though, to the phrase, "for so it seemed good in thy sight." If Jesus could pray those words when He was rejected, perhaps I could too. I wrote the words on a card and repeated them in my morning prayers. Throughout the day, I spoke the words out loud when I happened to glance toward the card, did dishes, or walked to the mailbox.

Slowly, praying those words made a difference. They ignited just enough hope to change my perspective. Perhaps in some deep, mysterious way God was accomplishing something in our lives that I couldn't begin to fathom or understand. With that little bit of hope, my inner strength returned enough where I could be an encouragement to Bob.

Whenever God is adored, reverenced, and worshiped, even when we don't feel like doing so, we give Him a channel in which to manifest Himself. As the Bible reminds us, God "inhabitest the praises" of His people (Psalm 22:3 KJV).

Those praises are like a few raindrops on hard, parched soil—the soil encasing our hope. That hard soil begins to crack and soften; hope starts to rise. Our outlook changes. We begin to believe life can get better, not because of who we are but because of who God is.

DON'T JUST STAND THERE, HELP SOMEONE

Pray for each other so that you may be healed.

—JAMES 5:16 NIV

As we discussed yesterday, Hebrews 13:15 encourages us to "always offer praise to God." Immediately after that exhortation, the writer of Hebrews follows with more words about sacrifice. He says, "Do not forget to do good and to help one another, because these are the sacrifices that please God" (v. 16). In addition, doing good and helping others offers a way to sprinkle raindrops on the hard, parched soil that encases our hope.

When God was helping Job with his difficult circumstances, He vindicated Job by chiding his friends because they did not speak the truth about Him the way Job had. He told Job to intercede and make offerings for his friends. Now that would be hard to do! Job's friends insisted and argued that Job, who was innocent, must have sinned to have so many catastrophes befall him. But "when Job prayed for his friends, the Lord restored his wealth and happiness!" (Job 42:10 TLB). I like the way the King James Version of the Bible says it, "The LORD turned the captivity of Job, when he prayed for his friends" (Job 42:10). Depression feels like captivity!

James also connects praying for others with healing. He said, "Confess your faults to one another, and pray one for another, that ye may be healed" (James 5:16 KJV). If we confess and talk about what we are dealing with to someone else, listen to their stories, and pray for and with each other, our depression may be affected because it takes the focus off our needs.

In Paul's thinking, even using our depression experience can help others. Paul shared his troubles with the Corinthians—the ones "so heavy" that he "felt that the death sentence had been passed on" him (2 Corinthians 1:8, 9). He said that God "helps us in all our troubles, so that we are able to help others who have all kinds of troubles" (v. 4).

There's something about our being concerned about others that lessens our self-concern and self-focus. If we can take some kind of action to help them, all the better. We'll be moving toward recovery.

John Kralik shares his experience of life transformation in his book *365 Thank Yous*. His action didn't necessarily focus on others at the onset, but it turned out that way. At 53, his life was far from what he always thought it would be. His law firm was failing, and he was facing divorce for the second time. He was overweight, distant from his older children, and afraid he might lose contact with his young daughter. All the while, he lived in a tiny, poorly ventilated apartment. His life dreams had slipped beyond his reach.

Determined to be grateful for the good in his life, Kralik set out to write 365 thank-you notes over the next year—to be his "way out of despair."

As he got into writing thank-you notes (one each day), he found "the murk of [his] fear, upset, and self-pity seemed to dissipate, and [he] often felt a little better" partly due to the fact, he claims, that he was focused on other people's lives instead of his own. This changed his life. His finances improved, he found true friendship, he lost weight, and best of all, he found inner peace.

In Byron Janis's case, it was writing music at the request of his wife that turned the tide for him. A world-renowned concert pianist, Janis wrote an article titled "Music for Troubled Souls" in the *Wall Street Journal* about how doing something for his wife, Maria, helped his depression begin to lift.

After a botched operation on his arthritic left thumb —something devastating to a concert pianist—he became depressed. One day his wife asked him to compose a theme for a documentary on her father, the actor Gary Cooper. Though Janis didn't feel up to it, he agreed.

When Janis played the theme for his wife, she suddenly began to cry. When Janis asked his wife why she was crying, she replied, "Because your music totally captures my father's spirit."

In reflecting on this moment in the article, Janis said, "It also recaptured me! That wonderful feeling of hope was coming back, and my depression slowly began to lift."

Patrick J. Kennedy, a mental health advocate who suffers from bipolar depression, tells in his book, *A Common Struggle*, about working a suicide hotline. He wrote, "While I suppose, deep inside, I did understand that the people I was talking to and trying to help were like me in some way, I mostly did this to get out of myself and as an educational adventure. I wanted to have this window into suffering that I couldn't make sense of myself." However, he also felt "a great sense of satisfaction doing it." He said, "I never left that room without feeling like I had in some way helped someone."

Praying for others and helping them takes the attention off our problems and ourselves and directs our attention toward others. It may bring long-term relief like it did for Job and Kralik, or it may be a temporary lessening of inner pressure like it was for Kennedy. Working a suicide hotline wasn't going to cure his bipolar depression, but for the moment, the intensity lessened as he experienced the gratification that comes with helping others.

Helping others isn't a tool that helps everyone overcome depression. It probably wouldn't have helped Moses. Helping people was the cause of his problems! He needed a different kind of solution—one God gave him. Helping someone else, though, is something all of us need to keep in mind. We need to be aware there are many tools available for us to make use of, depending on our situation. Or to put it another way, helping others makes for more raindrops that we can throw on the soil that encloses our hope.

WHEN IT ALL
COMES TOGETHER

May the God of all grace . . . settle you.

—1 Peter 5:10 NKJV

ARY Esther's husband, Tate, was patient when she began showing signs of being depressed. She cried a lot and couldn't seem to get anything done. She stopped going out and wouldn't respond to phone calls from friends. Tate grew concerned, especially when he made appointments for her to see their family doctor, and she either broke the appointment or didn't show up.

When Mary Esther started spending almost all her time in bed, Tate realized something had to be done. He said to her, "I'm worried about you, and I want to see you get better. This depression doesn't seem like it is going to lift on its own. I'm calling our doctor and asking him to admit you to our hospital's stress unit."

Mary Esther was appalled at the idea, and yet something deep within her said, "It's the right thing to do."

When she entered the stress unit, though, she wished she had never agreed to be admitted. She was certain she wasn't like any of the others there. Many were staring mindlessly at a TV, not really seeing the picture. Some walked aimlessly up and down the halls, and she could hear moaning in some of the rooms. One patient sat near the wall where he could repeatedly bang his head.

Not only did she wish she had never come, but she also wasn't interested in cooperating with the unit psychiatrist who spent time with her every day. She resisted taking the prescribed medication, but she did after much cajoling. She didn't want to participate in group therapy, but she finally agreed because the nurses insisted.

One day when Tate visited her, she asked him to bring a robe the next time he visited.

When Tate brought the robe, she was disappointed. It wasn't the one she had in mind. The one he brought she didn't often wear. After Tate left, she snuggled into the robe. It felt good, reminded her of home, and took away the chilliness.

The next day when she wore the robe again, she found a slip of paper in one of the pockets. *Hmm. What's this?*

She opened the slip, and on it was printed this Bible verse: "May the God of all grace, who called us to His eternal glory by Christ Jesus, after you have suffered a while, perfect, establish, strengthen, and settle you" (1 Peter 5:10 NKJV).

She was startled by the verse. She was startled by its presence. She had no idea how it got in her pocket, but she was also startled by the verse itself. She couldn't remember ever noticing this verse before. Sometimes it happens that way with Scripture. A verse will jump out at you with a freshness and clarity as if you have never read it before, and yet you know you must have.

She put the slip of paper back in her pocket but later pulled it out and read the verse again. The next day when she read it, she surprised herself by deciding to try to memorize it. She, whose mind had been unable even to remember appointments, was going to tackle learning this verse. As she did, she claimed this verse as God's message to her.

While other patients worked puzzles, she worked on memorizing. When she took her daily medications, she repeated 1 Peter 5:10. She said the verse out loud before she ate her meals. When she went to bed, she repeated it before turning off the light.

A week later, her psychiatrist said to Tate, "Mary Esther is making some progress. I think it would help her if you would take her away from the unit for a while. I don't mean back home. She's not ready to pick up life as she once knew it, but a relaxing, nonthreatening environment might help her grow stronger at this point."

They went to a remote place in the mountains where they could be alone and soak in the beauty of God's creation.

After they were there for a couple of days, Tate wanted to hike, but Mary Esther wasn't up to it. She encouraged him to go ahead without her.

While he was gone, she took in the scene around her. She listened to the birds and breathed in the fresh air. The place was serene, and she began to feel more serene. She also became more spiritually alert, something she hadn't experienced in a long time. She sensed God was "settling her" as the promise of 1 Peter 5:10 indicated He would. She could feel depression lifting and peace taking its place.

When Tate returned from his walk, she said, "I'm ready to get back to the stress unit and cooperate with the treatment plan. I want to get back home, back to life as we once knew it." Her suffering was coming to an end.

Some of you reading this may think I've shared Mary Esther's story to emphasize the importance of Scripture memory as a tool to fight depression. It is a tool and a good one—one not mentioned so far in this book. As important, though, as memorizing the Bible verse was to Mary Esther's recovery, her wellness cannot be attributed to just that verse.

The hospitalization, the medication, her husband's support, counseling with the psychiatrist, group therapy, being outdoors, and her spiritual awakening also contributed. At home, while her mind was foggy, she might have found the slip of paper and, thinking it trash, thrown it away. But in the stress unit she was experiencing some relief, taking medication, expressing emotions, and dealing with her thoughts in group therapy. Finding the Bible verse when she did was "the God of all grace" working all these things together to bring about Mary Esther's recovery (see Romans 8:28). For most of us, recovery from depression won't be simple. Most of us will need multiple tools to come to a moment of "settlement" after we "have suffered a while."

DAY 28

HOW YOU RESPOND MATTERS

Why this turmoil within me?

—Psalms 42:5, 11; 43:5 HCSB

THE day came for me when, like Mary Esther, I was "settled." That little green sprout of hope had turned into a healthy, growing plant. The depression was gone.

Intrigued by all that had happened, I began reading about depression. In the process, I made some discoveries that helped me understand why I became depressed while my husband didn't. We both experienced the same things. This discovery also helped me cultivate a depression-resistant lifestyle, something I continually work at.

One of the discoveries I made—and the one that has helped me the most—is that people usually have a habitual style of attempting to regulate their moods in reaction to stress. The two predominant styles are ruminators and distracters.

A ruminator is someone who turns a matter over and over in his or her mind like a cow who chews its cud over and over. We take the stress we are experiencing and repeatedly view it from different angles. We analyze the stress and try to determine why it happened and what it might mean. We focus on possible consequences and draw conclusions.

Ruminating may have been what the psalmist was doing when he asked repeatedly, "Why this turmoil within me?" (Psalms 42:5, 11; 43:5 HCSB). Ruminating makes for inner turmoil.

Perhaps Jeremiah was a ruminator. That would explain why the first 15 chapters of his prophecy are hard to understand. His thoughts are difficult to follow as he struggles with God's purpose for his life and the difficulties of the job God called him to do.

Solomon sounds like he could have been a ruminator. Throughout the Book of Ecclesiastes, there is the repetitive statement: "Vanity of vanities! All is vanity" (1:2 NASB). This is like saying, "Life is really empty," or, "Life is useless, all useless." This expression reveals Solomon's bleak outlook at life not turning out like he expected.

Ruminating isn't entirely bad. If Solomon were a ruminator, his ability to chew on observations and experiences probably contributed to his role as a wisdom teacher. Ruminating makes for being a good student of the Bible, for meditating, for thinking through problems, and for studying and organizing information. It's when the thoughts that replay themselves over and over are negative that ruminating contributes to depression and suffocates hope.

Distracters, on the other hand, respond to stress by diverting their attention. They act rather than reflect. They focus more on solutions, are more apt to think in alternatives, and, consequently, are less likely to become depressed.

I'm a ruminator, and my husband is a distracter. This would explain why I got upset when I felt the church was rejecting us, and Bob didn't. It also explains why when Bob went to work at a job outside of his field, I went to work trying to figure out what happened. When it made no sense, I concluded God did not have a purpose for our lives, and then I ruminated over that! If I were going to develop a depression-resistant lifestyle, I was going to have to learn to be more of a distracter.

This was not a simple thing to do. The force of habit is still there, still exerting its influence, but I try. Here are some things I do to distract myself and stop ruminating:

Change locations. This mostly means leaving the house and going somewhere else. For me, if this were leaving to take a walk by myself, it probably wouldn't work because I could still ruminate while walking!

Worship. I find that engaging in meaningful worship experiences helps. It must be worship so engaging that I switch my focus from self to God.

Visit a nursing home. The visit must include interacting with patients; otherwise, visiting a nursing home might add to my pessimistic ruminating.

Watch a movie. Movies can cast gloom over us as well as lighten our mood. For me to use a movie to break the power of ruminating, it must be one that makes me laugh or inspires me to take action.

I realize these actions are not applicable to all situations. If you've lost a loved one, then you wouldn't go to a movie or participate in group exercise to handle your shock and grief. A death deserves contemplation. But if ruminating goes on for an extended period of time, then it might be advisable to find some ways to distract your thoughts.

While it is challenging to do, learning to ruminate less gives us more confidence and keeps us from being overwhelmed by the stress we are experiencing. We increase our chances for control, reduce our sense of helplessness, and increase our hope.

Distracting doesn't mean we forget the problem, the pressures, the stress, or the words that prompted us to ruminate in the first place. But when we distract ourselves, we reduce the pressure and the emotions associated with it. We see what we are dealing with more clearly and objectively. The problem isn't as overwhelming. This is true for the person who is depressed and for the person who wants to resist becoming depressed.

THE POWER OF
"BUT" AND "YET"

Be careful how you think;
your life is shaped by your thoughts.

—PROVERBS 4:23

ANOTHER discovery I made that helps in maintaining a depression-resistant lifestyle is that thoughts govern our moods, not the other way around. The way we look at things—our perceptions, our mental attitudes, our beliefs, and our conclusions—regulate the way we feel.

The thoughts that lead to depression are usually ones that aren't quite accurate. Most people have distorted thinking of some kind.

The thoughts that lead to depression are ones that have a negative bent and are often critical in nature. *I'm no good. I'm a complete failure. I always make mistakes. Nothing ever works out for me. I can't do anything right. Nobody likes me. Everybody hates me.*

These accusations misrepresent reality. Everyone has some good qualities; no one is absolutely no good. We do some things right, so we're not complete failures. Everybody hates you? That would be a lot of people. How do you know that? How could you verify that statement?

A depressed person doesn't make a negative statement just one time. If he or she did, then it probably wouldn't do any damage. Rather, these are distorted thoughts that replay themselves over and over in a person's head.

A depressed person may have been thinking these thoughts for so long that he or she is unaware of their presence. The thoughts occur automatically and as solid truth.

While mental health researchers started identifying categories of distorted thinking linked to depression in the late twentieth century, people have been thinking this way for a long time. Naomi and Elijah give us examples of not quite accurate thinking.

When Naomi arrived back in Bethlehem with her daughter-in-law Ruth, she said, "When I left here, I had plenty, but the LORD has brought me back without a thing" (Ruth 1:21). Actually she didn't have plenty when she left. Naomi and her husband were escaping a famine. She said she came back "without a thing." That was also incorrect. She had a valuable asset in Ruth, who was with her as she said this.

When Elijah told God how unfaithful his fellow Israelites had been, he said, "I am the only one left" (1 Kings 19:10, 14), implying he was the only one faithful to God. God reminded Elijah there 7,000 other faithful Israelites (v. 18)!

Up until I did this research, it never occurred to me something might be wrong with my thinking. My thoughts were certainly logical and accurate to me! The more I read, though, the more I became convinced I needed to pay attention to my thoughts and evaluate them.

Sometimes it meant working backwards. *I feel this way right now. What's caused me to think this way?* Once the thought was identified, I had to challenge it and replace it with truth.

If I had known to do this when I concluded that our church stamped us "unacceptable," I would have asked myself, *Is this really true? Did the whole church deem us unacceptable?* Probably not, as we were in a very large church. What exactly did *unacceptable* mean? That we couldn't serve in a paid position anywhere? Did this mean we were totally without influence? Weren't people still coming to the Sunday School classes we taught? And most importantly, weren't we still acceptable to God? There were other churches in which we could serve. I was categorically discounting us because I took personally our church's not hiring my husband as missions pastor. I replayed the "unacceptable" theme over and over, and in doing so, prepared the soil for growing depression.

How much better it would have been to quench the "unacceptable" label immediately rather than let it lead to sadness and disappointment. Thoughts can be changed! As the Apostle Paul reminds us, thoughts can be taken captive and dealt with (see 2 Corinthians 10:5). One way he did this was by using the words "but" and "yet." Paul dealt with many rejections and difficulties that could have easily discouraged another person. He remained strong by stating the positive.

> *We felt that the death sentence had been passed on us.* But *this happened so that we should rely, not on ourselves,* but *only on God.*
> —*2 Corinthians 1:9, author's emphasis*

> *We are often troubled,* but *not crushed; sometimes in doubt,* but *never in despair; there are many enemies,* but *we are never without a friend; and though badly hurt at times, we are not destroyed.*
> —*2 Corinthians 4:8–9, author's emphasis*

> *We are treated as liars,* yet *we speak the truth; as unknown,* yet *we are known by all; as though we were dead,* but, *as you see, we live on. Although punished, we are not killed; although saddened, we are always glad; we seem poor,* but *we make many people rich; we seem to have nothing,* yet *we really possess everything.*
> —*2 Corinthians 6:8–10, author's emphasis*

Paul used "but" and "yet" to counter each negative with a positive, not allowing hardship to dampen his hope.

This is an example of something we can do. When insults, trials, and disappointments come our way, we can say or write a positive rebuttal to each negative thought that surfaces. This will keep us from developing negative feelings that might erode our hope. With two little powerful words, "but" and "yet," we can keep our hope alive and thriving.

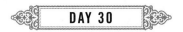

DAY 30

WHEN HOPE THRIVES

*The LORD blessed the latter end of Job
more than his beginning.*

—JOB 42:12 KJV

A FTER Job prayed for his friends, God prospered him with greater blessings than he had known before his many losses and subsequent depression. He fathered more children and enjoyed four generations of offspring until he died "full of years," offering proof that there is life after depression.

Amy Bleuel wanted people struggling with depression, suicide, or addiction to believe their struggle was not the end, but a beginning. This desire came out of her own experience of abuse, life in the foster care system, and her father's suicide when Bleuel was 18. She wanted to memorialize her father, and she wanted to share how her faith, friends, and family helped her overcome depression. She set up a website, shared her experience, and invited others to tell their stories. Bleuel encouraged people to draw a semicolon on their wrists as a reminder that whatever they may be experiencing, it was only a pause along life's way.

On ProjectSemicolon.org, it says, "A semicolon is used when an author could've ended a sentence but chose not to. You are the author, and the sentence is your life."

People who experience depression may feel like it's the end, that things will never be right or bright again. But it doesn't have to be that way. What happens to us doesn't have to be a final period; rather, it can be a hope-filled semicolon indicating better days ahead.

Does the semicolon appeal to you as a symbol? It is a meaningful one, but perhaps you would prefer a more tangible symbol such as a cross to carry in your pocket, wear around your neck, or attach to your key chain. As you feel the cross, rubbing it between your fingers, it could remind you of Jesus' words, "I am the resurrection and the life" (John 11:25).

Jesus said those words to Martha when he returned to Bethany after receiving the news that Lazarus was sick. By the time Jesus arrived, Lazarus had died and was buried in a tomb. With His words, "I am the resurrection and the life," Jesus was assuring Martha he could offer life where there appeared to be no life. Those words have meaning far beyond bringing Lazarus physically back to life. They speak to bringing people back to life spiritually, such as someone who has been wrapped in the grave clothes of depression.

While both the semicolon and cross are meaningful symbols, the one that works best for me with regard to depression is a green fern. My symbol has to be something alive, green, and growing.

That plumosa fern—that one that sprouted due to some raindrops—is long gone. It got left behind in a move. Yes, we moved again when my husband got a job back in his field. My life continued, but it continued with a different quality because of what I learned in dealing with depression.

I still don't understand why my husband and I experienced what we did. I do know, though, that God is alive and working through me, and that He has a purpose for my life. Unlike the semicolon or the cross, my symbol has to be watered and fertilized. Every day in my prayertime, I water and feed my soul. I acknowledge—out loud—that God has a purpose for my life and read what He has to say to me in His Word.

I've learned how to recognize depression and how to deal with it. I never knew what depression was until I was diagnosed. Looking back at those "before I knew" years, I could see dips in the road that were close to being depressive episodes. A pattern was developing. Apparently I have a predisposition toward depression, so learning how to ward it off has made my life better than it would have been otherwise.

My experience has made me stronger, and, according to Peter, that's how it is supposed to work when we are believers. He wrote, "After you have suffered for a little while, the God of all grace . . . will himself perfect you and give you firmness, strength, and a sure foundation" (1 Peter 5:10). I have that indelible picture planted in my brain and heart of Jesus holding on to me when I was ready to let go. Jesus keeps my lamp burning, burning, burning.

Most importantly, at least with regard to my mental health, I've learned the importance of hope and how to nurture it. I no longer take hope for granted as I once did. I don't assume it will just "be there" in my life. Rather, I recognize it as a necessary force for vibrant living, and so I do what I can to see that hope thrives in my life, and it does. I trust hope thrives in your life as well.

> *May God, the source of hope, fill you with all joy and peace by means of your faith in him, so that your hope will continue to grow by the power of the Holy Spirit.*
> *—Romans 15:13*

APPENDIX

Signs That You May Be Suffering from Depression

Are you feeling sad or down in the dumps *or* have you lost interest in life and things you used to enjoy?

Everyone feels sad or disinterested at times, but usually it is temporary. In depression, the feelings persist. The American Psychiatric Association's *Diagnostic and Statistical Manual of Mental Disorders* describes depression as having at least five of the following nine symptoms for *more than two weeks*. If you answer yes to *five* or *more* of the following symptoms, then you may be depressed.

1. Have your sleeping patterns changed? Insomnia or sleeping too much?
2. Have your eating habits changed? Eating more or eating less?
3. Are you feeling fatigued, tired, run-down, and without your usual energy or motivation?
4. Are you having trouble concentrating, thinking, remembering, or deciding?
5. Have you been unable to sit still to the point where it is necessary to be moving about constantly? Or do you feel like it is too much trouble to move about?
6. Are you more prone to irritability or feelings of discouragement and pessimism?
7. Are you feeling guilty, worthless, or down on yourself?
8. Are you no longer enjoying things you once found enjoyment in?
9. Have you been preoccupied by thoughts of taking your own life or by wishing you were dead? (If your answer to this last question is yes, you need to go immediately to the nearest hospital emergency room. You will either be given a suicide assessment there, or they will send you to another hospital that does this type of assessment and can also provide treatment.)

When to Seek Professional Help

While this book recommends many self-help tools for dealing with depression, there may be times when you need to seek professional help. Here are some signs that it would be best for you to seek the help of your primary care doctor, a psychiatrist, a psychologist, a licensed professional counselor, a social worker, or your pastor.

You don't know what caused your depression. The black cloud of despair hovering over you came out of nowhere, seemingly without cause, and feels dark and foreboding.

You can't sleep or you're sleeping most of the time.

You are losing a serious amount of weight.

You are experiencing severe physical discomfort that is affecting your overall health.

This is not your first depressive episode. You are having repeated bouts of depression.

Your depression is hurting your marriage, your family, or your job.

Your depression is so heavy that *no* self-help tool brings you relief of any kind.

You are having suicidal thoughts. In this case, you need immediate medical attention. Contact your doctor right away or go to the nearest hospital emergency room.

Give a GIFT OF HOPE

The "Gifts of Hope" series offers hope to those walking through some of life's most challenging circumstances. Each book offers 30 devotionals, Scripture, and prayers that provide readers inspiration and encouragement.

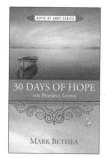
N154115
$9.99 plus s&h

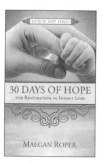
N154116
$9.99 plus s&h

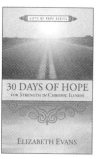
N164105
$9.99 plus s&h

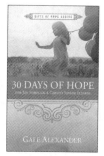
N164115
$9.99 plus s&h

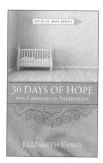
N164104
$9.99 plus s&h

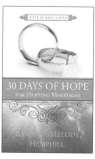
N174106
$9.99 plus s&h

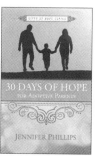
N174113
$9.99 plus s&h

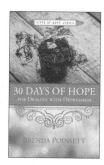
N174118
$9.99 plus s&h

Visit **NewHopePublishers.com** to learn more about the "Gifts of Hope" series, read sample chapters, and more.

New Hope® Publishers is a division of WMU®, an
international organization that challenges Christian believers
to understand and be radically involved in God's mission.
For more information about WMU, go to wmu.com.
More information about New Hope books
may be found at NewHopePublishers.com.
New Hope books may be purchased at your local bookstore.

Please go to
NewHopePublishers.com
for more helpful information about
30 Days of Hope for Dealing With Depression.

If you've been blessed by this book,
we would like to hear your story.
The publisher and author welcome your comments and
suggestions at: newhopereader@wmu.org.